The Institutions of
Liberal Democratic States

The Institutions of Liberal Democratic States

Munroe Eagles, Christopher Holoman, Larry Johnston

broadview press

Broadview Press, Ltd.

is an independent, international publishing house, incorporated in 1985.

We welcome any comments and suggestions regarding any aspect of our publications—please feel free to contact us at:

NORTH AMERICA

Post Office Box 1243,
Peterborough, Ontario,
Canada K9J 7H5
Tel: (705) 743-8990
Fax: (705) 743-8353

3576 California Road,
Orchard Park, New York
USA 14120

UK, IRELAND, AND
CONTINENTAL EUROPE

NBN Plymbridge Distributors, Ltd.
Estover Road
Plymouth PL6 7PY
UK
Tel: (01752) 202301
Fax: (01752) 202333
orders@nbnplymbridge.com

AUSTRALIA AND NEW ZEALAND

UNIREPS
University of New South Wales
Sydney, NSW, 2052
Tel: + 61 2 96640999
Fax: + 61 2 96645420
info.press@unsw.edu.au

broadview@broadviewpress.com
customerservice@broadviewpress.com
www.broadviewpress.com

Broadview believes in shared owner-ship, both with its employees and with the general public; since the year 2000 Broadview shares have traded publicly on the Toronto Venture Exchange under the symbol BDP.

Library and Archives Canada Cataloguing in Publication

Eagles, Donald Munroe, 1956–
    The institutions of liberal democratic states / Munroe Eagles, Christopher Holoman, Larry Johnston.

Previously published as: Politics : an introduction to democratic government.
Includes bibliographical references and index.
ISBN 1-55111-700-2

    1. Political science.   2. Democracy.   I. Holoman, Christopher, 1957–   II. Johnston, Lawrence Walker, 1955–   III. Title.

JA66.E34 2004a   320   C2004-903723-4

Book designed and typeset by Zack Taylor, www.zacktaylor.com.

Cover image © 2004 Photodisc Blue

This book is printed on 100% post-consumer recycled, ancient forest friendly paper.

Printed in Canada

CONTENTS

Chapter One **The State: Constitutions, Institutions, and Systems** 7

1.1 Introduction 7
1.2 Functions of the State 8
1.3 Constitutions and Constitutionalism 10
1.4 Institutions 17
    1.4.1 Legislatures 18
    1.4.2 Executives 20
    1.4.3 Judiciaries 24
1.5 Systems 26
    1.5.1 Separated Powers (Presidential Systems) 26
    1.5.2 Concentrated Powers (Parliamentary Systems) 31
    1.5.3 Comparing Systems 35

Chapter Two **Presidential versus Parliamentary Systems:**
Executives and Legislatures in Liberal Democracies 37

2.1 Introduction 37
2.2 Presidentialism Explored 38
2.3 Parliamentary Systems 44
    2.3.1 Majoritarian versus Proportionate Systems 46
    2.3.2 Majority, Minority, and Coalition Government 49
    2.3.3 Formation and Dissolution of Parliamentary
            Governments 52
    2.3.4 The Head of State 60
    2.3.5 The Political Executive: Prime Minister
            and Cabinet 61
    2.3.6 Policy-Making: Executive Dominance 63
2.4 Presidentialism in Parliamentary Systems:
    France as a Hybrid 67
2.5 Conclusion 70

Chapter Three   **Governing Territory: Unitary and Federal Systems**   73

    3.1   Introduction: Decentralization and Centralization   73
    3.2   Definitions: Federal, Confederal, and Unitary Systems   74
    3.3   Why Federalism?   75
    3.4   The Division of Powers   77
        3.4.1   Legislative Powers   78
        3.4.2   Administrative Powers   78
        3.4.3   Fiscal Powers   83
    3.5   Bicameralism in Federal States   85
    3.6   Home Rule and Decentralization in Unitary States   89
    3.7   Supranational Federalism: The European Union   91

Chapter Four   **Cleavage Structures and Electoral Systems**   97

    4.1   Cleavages Defined   97
    4.2   Some Cleavages Examined   99
        4.2.1   Religious   100
        4.2.2   Ethno-Linguistic   101
        4.2.3   Center-Periphery   101
        4.2.4   Urban-Rural   102
        4.2.5   Class   103
    4.3   Reinforcing and Cross-Cutting Cleavages   104
    4.4   Electoral Systems: The Basics   106
    4.5   Electoral Systems: Main Variants   110
        4.5.1   Single-Member (Majoritarian) Systems   113
        4.5.2   Proportionate Electoral Systems   117
        4.5.3   Hybrid (Mixed-Member) Systems   123
    4.6   Party Systems   124
    4.7   Conclusion   129

    Index   133

ONE | # The State:
Constitutions, Institutions, and Systems

... the state is a human community that (successfully) claims the
monopoly of the legitimate use of physical force in a given territory.
— Max Weber, "*Politics as a Vocation*," 1919

This chapter briefly introduces the main functions all states are presumed to perform, and identifies the key institutional arrangements that liberal democracies have adopted to perform these functions. Subsequent chapters will elaborate on the basic patterns identified here.

As societies attain a sufficient size and complexity, they develop the permanent bureaucratic structure we associate with the state. The liberal democratic version of the state is in part a byproduct of the depersonalization of power and authority that reflects dissatisfaction with late feudal forms of government, such as absolute monarchy. Depersonalizing government means relying on institutions and processes (i.e., rule-governed procedures) rather than on the arbitrary decisions of individuals. We need to recall that one of the purposes—if not *the* purpose—of government is to provide order and stability, a certain coherence and predictability to the interactions of members of a society. As these societies continue to expand and become more diverse, mobile, and technologically driven, the ordering activity of government *necessarily* relies increasingly on institutions and processes, or, on increasingly sophisticated institutions and processes. In short, as society (and life within society) becomes more complicated, so, too, must government (or, in its place the institutions of civil society).

1.1
Introduction

1.1   Introduction
1.2   Functions of the State
1.3   Constitutions and
       Constitutionalism
1.4   Institutions
       1.4.1   Legislatures
       1.4.2   Executives
       1.4.3   Judiciaries
1.5   Systems
       1.5.1   Separated
                Powers
                (Presidential
                Systems)
       1.5.2   Concentrated
                Powers
                (Parliamentary)
       1.5.3   Comparing
                Systems

Within the wide diversity of states and the multiplicity of constitutions that define them, a few basic functions are common, and indeed it is arguable that such functions must be performed in some way in any political society. It is important to keep distinct the **FUNCTIONS** governments perform, from the **INSTITUTIONS** that perform them, and both of these distinct from the type of system or **CONSTITUTION** that arranges the institutions and their relationships.

Part of all Democracies

1.2 Functions of the State

The classic threefold distinction we will begin with revolves around three different aspects of one inescapable fact: governments *decide*—this is what it means to have power, to be authoritative. In all collective enterprises, short of achieving unanimity, someone or some group must decide for the rest *and* do so in such a way that the rest acknowledge their right to do so. The most basic function of the state, then, is one of **DECISION-MAKING**. Because authority is now generally exercised through the impersonal instrument of law, the decision-making function is often called the **LEGISLATIVE** function, "legislating" being the business of making laws. We should recognize that the decisions made by government may be quite different from law. On the one hand, whereas laws are rules that apply more or less universally and continually, some decisions (e.g., to appoint an ambassador, to declare a national disaster, to recognize a citizen's outstanding bravery) may be one-time and quite particular. On the other hand, while laws are generally statements about what may or may not be done, or about what must or must not be done (i.e., they permit or prohibit, prescribe or proscribe), many authoritative decisions are about conferring benefits (like pensions) or providing public goods (like education or health care), or encouraging economic activity (through subsidies, loans, or setting interest rates, etc.). Most of us meet government more often through these kinds of programs than by encountering "the law." In this sense, the decision-making function is broader than law, and is better captured by the term "policy-making." **POLICY** in turn can be defined broadly as *any course of action or inaction that government deliberately chooses to take.*

In any organized society, decisions—whether particular, regulatory, or programmatic—must be made in an authoritative way. Institutions, processes, and the systems that organize both will determine at least three things:

gov'ts decide

1. *who* will make these decisions,
2. *how* these decisions will be made, and

3. *what* decisions can or cannot in fact be made.

These three variables, the "who," "how," and "what" of deci-sion-making, will vary considerably from polity to polity, or even more so, from type of political system to type of political system. As might be equally obvious, these variables also will apply to other functions of the state.

To make a decision is one thing; to implement it or carry it out is another matter altogether. It is probably safe to say that most of us are better at making decisions than at realizing them, and that most of us would rather make decisions than implement them, given the choice. Nonetheless, if decisions are not somehow put into effect, they become meaningless. Just as the kinds of deci-sions governments make can vary, so, too, will implementation of decisions. In the case of a law, it may mean enforcing sanctions or penalties against those who do not obey; with a policy or broad program it may involve the delivery of services, or the payment of funds, or the maintenance of a physical plant, etc. In either case, a complex organization of resources, human and otherwise, is required to carry out what was intended in the authoritative decision. This function is typically called the **EXECUTIVE** or admin-istrative function of the state. By and large this is entrusted to the permanent bureaucracy that characterizes the state as a form of social organization. Modern government consists to a large degree of many bureaucracies, organized to deliver programs, enforce laws, or administer regulations. Collectively, these various government departments that implement decisions are sometimes called "the bureaucracy."

Finally, wherever authoritative decisions are made and imple-mented, there will be disputes, and the kinds of disagreement will be as various as the decisions and their implementation. Consider the "who," "how," and "what" of decision-making again—each of these is a possible source of dispute. Was the decision made by the person or body authorized to make such decisions? Was the decision made according to the procedural rules set out for decision-makers? Was the decision one that can in fact be made by decision-makers? Someone or some body must have the respon-sibility for answering these questions or settling these disputes—if not, the legitimacy of the state could be undermined. This function of adjudication, or dispute settlement, has commonly been called the **JUDICIAL** function and is conducted by the **JUDICIARY**.

Judgment of disputes concerning the authoritative decisions of the state usually falls into one of two very broad categories:

disputes about the decision itself (as the examples in the previous paragraph illustrate), or about the implementation of the decision. Roughly (and only roughly) this corresponds to a distinction between matters of law, and matters of fact. Most criminal and many civil cases, for example, are of the latter kind: what must be judged is the guilt, innocence, or liability of the accused party; the law itself is not at issue. In most constitutional cases, by contrast, what is in dispute is the law itself, its validity, or, in many cases, its meaning. Here judgment is primarily about *interpretation*. As with decision-making, so, too, for decision-adjudicating, there are variations with respect to who adjudicates, how they adjudicate, and what they may adjudicate. If all societies require authoritative decisions and thus making them is a primary function of *all* governments (or states), then these societies will also require decisions to be implemented and disputes about decisions to be settled—the executive and judicial functions will be as basic to government as the legislative function. Various political thinkers have ascribed other functions to the state, and in most cases what these indicate are more specific ends or goals that governments provide or seek to accomplish. These purposes or goods are in fact what governments use their decision-making and implementing power to accomplish. These particular goods or functions that constitute the business of the state will vary considerably according to the type of society, the level of technology, period in history, etc. For example, we might say that it is a function of governments to ensure that citizens achieve an adequate level of education; 200 years ago few, if any, governments would have recognized such a task as their responsibility. On the other hand, defense of citizens and their possessions from aggression, internal or external, has been recognized as a purpose of the state probably as long as there have been states (see also Figure 1.1).

1.3 Constitutions and Constitutionalism

Perhaps the most basic distinction to be drawn in comparative politics is between constitutional and non-constitutional governments. We might define a constitution as *a body of fundamental or basic rules* (indeed, the German constitution is called the Basic Law) *outlining the structures of power and authority and the relations between these, and between these and the people.* In short, constitutions are a set of basic rules that make the exercise of political power regulatory and non-arbitrary. Laws that politicians make that stand in opposition to the legal provisions of a constitution can be struck down by the legal system and declared illegal in a process called **JUDICIAL REVIEW** (see below).

We do well to remember that as law, this written constitution is really a map or diagram purporting to outline the fundamental nature of the state as it exists and operates. Normally, but not necessarily, these rules are codified in a written text. What Walter Bagehot (1870) called "the English Constitution" was not a written document, but rather the actual structure of the power and authority of the English state. In this sense, "the English constitution" is unusual among modern democracies; it is (or is described as) "unwritten." In other words, there is no single document regarded as the English constitution, although several documents (like the Magna Carta, the Statute of Westminster, etc.) have constitutional significance because they describe key relationships between institutions of state, or between the state and the people. It is no accident, then, that the British state is probably the most unlimited of modern democracies. As the 2nd Earl of Pembroke once said, "A parliament can do any thing but make a man a woman, and a woman a man." There are important senses in which this remains true, particularly if the government has public opinion on its side.

By contrast, when Americans talk about the Constitution, a written document is being referred to, a body of law that serves like a legal blueprint for the edifice of the state. The distinction between British and American constitutions is based on whether constitutional rules are collected in a single written document. A more important distinction relating to constitutions exists, however. For example, the written constitution of the former Soviet Union would lead an uncritical reader to believe that citizens of that nondemocratic (and "non-constitutional") state were as well-protected and governed as in any genuine liberal democracy. The existence of constitutional documents, however, does not guarantee the existence of constitutional rule. This may be thought of as a distinction between the formal (written) constitution and the **MATERIAL CONSTITUTION** (the actual structure). Ideally, the formal describes the material. Just as a map becomes out of date when high seas wash away a coastline, or a dam floods a valley, so can parts of the written constitution cease to describe the reality of the state; just as maps are redrawn to reflect a changing world, constitutions sometimes must be rewritten to match new political realities.

To describe the idea that the state will be limited by a written constitution, we will use the term **CONSTITUTIONALISM**. Constitutionalism has several requirements. In addition to the rules that define what governments may or may not do (or how

FUNCTIONS OF THE STATE

FOUND IN ALL STATES

1. Population control: fixing of boundaries, establishment of citizenship categories, census taking.
2. Judiciary: laws, legal procedure, and judges.
3. Enforcement: permanent military and police forces.
4. Fiscal: taxation.
   — Kottak (1991: 129)

MAY ALL BE FOUND IN A SINGLE STATE, BUT NOT NECESSARILY, AND NOT IN SAME PRIORITY

1. Pattern maintenance: to keep in power those who have power, wealthy those who have wealth.
2. Organizing for conquest.
3. Pursuit of wealth.
4. The welfare state.
5. The mobilization state.
   — Deutsch (1990: 24-25)

FOUR MOST PERSISTENT TYPES OF STATE ACTIVITIES

1. The maintenance of internal order.
2. Military defense/ aggression, directed against foreign foes.
3. The maintenance of communications infrastructures.
4. Economic redistribution.
   — Mann (1990: 69)

FIGURE 1.1

they may or may not do it), there must be a forum where disputes about the meaning of the constitution and whether or not it has been adhered to can be heard and decided. This, we have seen, is the function of a high or "supreme" or special constitutional court. It follows that there should also be a means of enforcing constitutional rules and rulings. In theory this would mean some other institution of the state, such as police or military, willing to employ force on behalf of the authority of the supreme or constitutional court. In normal practice, if ever, constitutions don't work this way. Perhaps the most important facet of constitutionalism is its requirement that all political actors abide by the constitutional rules of the polity, and where these are in dispute, all recognize the legitimacy of the body designated for deciding these disputes, and abide by its rulings. We might call this disposition on the part of political actors a constitutional ethic or norm, and without it, constitutions will be merely symbolic documents. By analogy, when one agrees to play a game, one has also agreed to abide by the rules of that game, and accept the word of the duly constituted umpire if there are disputes about what is acceptable or not. You cannot, because a rule is contrary to your purposes, simply set it aside in the middle of the game. And yet, when a political leader "suspends" a constitution because of supposed "instability" when all that is threatened is his or her own electoral chances, that is all that has been done. In such a case there is a constitution, but no constitutionalism. Ultimately, constitutionalism cannot be forced, or enforced, but must become such an integral part of the political culture that political actors cannot conceive of doing other than as the constitution permits. This is one reason why it is important that the body of constitutional rules remain in touch with the central values, beliefs, and aspirations of the population of the polity.

The English (or rather British) constitution discussed above provides a good illustration of the normative character of constitutionalism. As noted, there is no single written body of rules that can be identified as the British constitution, nor is there a supreme or constitutional court that can deliver rulings binding on Parliament. In a strictly *legal* sense, the government of Britain faces no limits on its actions, it must only consider the *political* limits imposed by representative democracy. At the same time, there are numerous individual statutes, judicial rulings, and even unwritten rules that define political relationships between institutions of state, and between the British state and the people, and these function as constitutional rules in the absence of a body to enforce them *because the relevant political actors accept them as constitutional.* The choice between having a written constitution and no ethic of constitutionalism (as in the former U.S.S.R.) and having an ethic of constitutionalism but no written constitution (as in Britain) is not a difficult one to make.

The preceding discussion points out that constitutional rules can take many forms, varying in their level of formality and codification. Most obvious is written bodies of law identified as a constitution: the Constitution of the United States of America, Germany's Basic Law, Canada's Constitution Act. Sometimes these written constitutions are produced by legislatures, sometimes by a special assembly of delegates or representatives meeting for that purpose; whatever their origin they will (normally) be ratified by the legislatures of the political units involved and thus become the most basic part of the law of the land. In almost all cases, what distinguishes these constitutional statutes from ordinary law, apart from their subject matter, is that they are more difficult to change. Normally the written constitution will contain rules about how it is to be altered, an **AMENDING PROCEDURE**. This will stipulate a higher level of consent than the simple majority usually required to make law, or the consent of more than one legislature or institution, or popular ratification through a referendum, or some combination of these. Amending procedures must meet the challenge of being flexible enough to allow necessary change, while at the same time remaining rigid enough to guide or limit rulers. At the very least, it is expected that constitutional laws will be more difficult to change than ordinary laws, and for this reason we usually describe constitutional provisions that are so protected from change as *entrenched*.

Constitutional matters may also be addressed, particularly in countries without a written constitutional document, in ordinary law, or what are called **STATUTES**. Change to such laws is achieved through the rules and constraints of the legislative process. If a simple legislative majority is necessary to make a statute, then a similar majority will suffice to change or cancel it. In such cases, constitutional rules are under the control of the legislature, and this puts limitations on the ability, and hence the willingness, of the courts to engage in judicial review on the basis of such statutes; legislatures unhappy with judicial rulings will simply change the rules. In some legal systems, legal precedents from earlier constitutional disputes may also be a part of the constitution itself. This kind of law is made by judges in the Anglo-American legal tradition, what is known as **COMMON LAW**, articulated by magistrates through their verdicts and decisions. Sometimes called "judge-made law," common law builds on a tradition of previous cases by adhering to the rule of *stare decisis*, a commitment to abide by the example of previous decisions in similar cases, or what we commonly call **PRECEDENT**. The purpose of precedent is to avoid arbitrary decisions by treating common cases in a like manner, and in common law countries (like Britain, the U.S., Canada, Australia, and New Zealand) it can also have constitutional significance: constitutional rulings and interpretations will, like criminal and civil cases, be argued on the basis of past decisions, where applicable. Decisions handed down by the high or supreme court will serve as precedents for future cases of a similar nature. Common law is more flexible than statutes, but it is also subordinate to the latter; once a matter has been treated in a statute it has been removed from the sphere of common law.

The last kind of constitutional rule is what is called a **CONVENTION** (not to be confused with "constitutional conventions" used to draft and periodically revise constitutional documents), that is best understood as an unwritten rule that remains nonetheless binding, although the force that binds here is that of tradition, or morality, or expedience, and not a legal force. Conventions are more central than might sometimes be supposed. The judicial rule of abiding by precedents noted above is conventional, and the requirements of responsible government and of the fusion of powers, both discussed below, are also only conventions. Because conventions are unwritten rules, they are the least enforceable, and the most dependent among constitutional rules on the norm or ethic of constitutionalism for their force.

Of these four ways in which constitutional rules may be expressed—entrenched document, ordinary statute, common law, and convention—only the first two satisfy what is meant by a written constitution (i.e., formal constitution), but the material constitution of a state (i.e., constitution as institution) may be, and often is, expressed in a mixture of all four kinds of rules.

Last, but not least, we should consider the content of constitutional rules. As the fundamental rules of the polity, the rules that govern rulers and ruling, constitutions do the following, although not all constitutions will address all of these topics, or give equal stress to each of them:

1. Define who exercises authority and/or the institutions and processes by which authority is exercised, and in either case, what kind of authority (or function of the state) is involved. Examples of this would include indicating that the chief executive is an elected president, or that legislation must receive the support of a majority in both houses of the legislature, or the maximum time permissible between elections, or rules concerning the qualifications for holding office, etc.

2. Outline the relationships between and the priority of the various primary institutions and offices (or branches) of the state. The various checks and balances of the American system of separated powers would fall in this category, as would the fusion of powers of the parliamentary model, if constitutionalized. The relationship of the head of state to other fundamental institutions may be addressed here, or the relationship of a strong president to a prime minister in a system like that of France or Poland.

Both (1) and (2) cover the basic elements of systems or types of constitution, discussed above. In addition, constitutions may (but do not necessarily) address the following:

3. If applicable, divide jurisdictions between levels of government, and define other fundamental relationships between them. This is a necessary task in federal states, and we will discuss what this means at greater length in Chapter 3.

4. Establish the rights of citizens with respect to the state, and indicate how they may seek redress for violation of these rights. The first ten amendments to the U.S. Constitution comprise what is known as the Bill of Rights. Criticism of the British constitution for its lack of enshrining such "positive rights" for it citizens has been growing. Since 1988 there has been a vigorous campaign in that country pressing for the adoption of a constitutionally-entrenched (and hence legally protected) Bill of Rights. Canada is one state with a "constitution similar in principle to that of the United Kingdom" but as part of a series of constitutional changes in 1982, the country adopted a Charter of Rights and Freedoms. Inevitably, the likelihood and extent of judicial review is greatly enhanced by the presence of an entrenched rights code, and this has enormous significance for the operation of the political system.

5. Indicate the conditions that must be satisfied to amend the constitution. In general, because constitutional rules are considered more basic and fundamental than other types of legal and political directives, constitutional changes are more difficult to achieve than other forms. Amending formulas may be simple or complex, and they may be rigid or flexible, and there is no necessary link between these two dimensions. The American amendment process is fairly simple, but turns out in practice to be rigid; over 10,000 amendments have been proposed since 1787, but only 26 have passed (ten of which constituted the Bill of Rights, and were passed in 1789). As might be expected, a constitutional amendment can be proposed at the federal level or at the state level. In the former case a proposal must receive a two-thirds vote in both houses of Congress. In the latter instance, a proposal may be made by a national convention called for that purpose if requested by two-thirds (34) of the 50 states. In fact, this latter method of proposal has never been used. Once proposed, an amendment must be *ratified*, which requires approval by three-quarters of the states, either approval by the state legislatures, or by constitutional conventions held in the states. It is up to Congress to choose the method of ratification, and ratification by conventions was used only once (to end Prohibition). It should perhaps also be noted that at each stage, by either means, the margin of approval is much greater than a simple majority; this is common to constitutional votes and reflects the belief that the basic rules should not be constantly changing.

By contrast, the Basic Law of Germany has a simple and flexible amending procedure: a vote of two-thirds of the members of both houses of the federal legislature. In this case, the provision that the members of the *Bundesrat* (upper house) are delegates of the *Länder* (i.e., state or provincial) governments makes such a simple procedure capable of securing the consent of both levels of state. As a result it has been possible for the German constitution, although less than 50 years old, to be amended with great frequency. Interestingly, though, there are parts of the German constitution that cannot be amended, including the existence of a federal system, and some fundamental individual rights.

Australia and Switzerland, each in their own way, provide examples of federal systems where the people have a direct role in the constitutional amendment process. In Australia, the normal procedure is for a proposal to receive a majority in both Houses of Parliament, and then be submitted to the people for ratification through a referendum. In cases where a proposal passes one House but not the other, it may, if passed a second time by the original chamber, be submitted by the Governor-General to the public in a referendum. To succeed, a proposal must receive a majority of all votes cast in the country, as well as a majority of the votes cast in a majority of the states (i.e., a "double majority"). In Switzerland the procedures by which a proposal may be put to the chambers of Parliament and/or to the people are much more complicated, and complicated by the possibility that a full or partial revision of the constitution may be requested by a portion of the public. At the end of the day, though, Swiss constitutional change requires popular ratification and, as in Australia, it must receive a double majority: a national majority, and a majority in a majority of the cantons.

On this matter as in others, the Canadian experience is rather unusual. For 115 years amendment of much of the Canadian constitution, and certainly anything touching upon a dimension of federalism, could only be done by the Parliament of Great Britain. Canada's original written constitution, the British North America Act of 1867, was an act of the British parliament, and as such, could be changed only by an act of that legislature. In time, the convention developed that the British government would change the Canadian constitution only at the request of Canadian governments, and there were any number of occasions (including any time after the Statute of Westminster of 1931) when the British government would have gladly turned over the Canadian constitution to Canadian governments. The stumbling block remained the inability of the Canadian government and the provincial governments to agree on an amending formula, and this despite several serious attempts in the postwar period to find an acceptable solution. The history of these attempts and the reasons why success was finally achieved in 1982 indicates how complex and difficult it is to secure agreement concerning the rules of the game in a divided country. As in the United States and Germany, and unlike Switzerland and Australia, constitutional amendment in Canada (at least according to the constitution) is a matter for governments, not the direct decision of the people. In some cases governments can act alone. In other cases, the national government and one or more states/provinces may act together in ways that affect only themselves. In all cases, however, constitutional change is, by design, difficult to obtain.

Regardless of their form, constitutions have a common function: to provide a fundamental definition of the structures and processes of authority. **DECISION-MAKING**, **IMPLEMENTATION**, and **ADJUDICATION** are common to all political communities that have a state and the alternative designation of these functions as the legislative, executive, and judicial functions indicates a relationship with the primary institutions responsible for performing these functions in the modern state. Whether functions are named for institutions or vice versa is a moot point. It is important to appreciate that this division is relatively modern, and that the correspondence of functions and institutions is not always as direct as may first appear.

Consider classical times. While the Greeks distinguished between democracy, aristocracy, and monarchy as types of constitutions or systems, common to all was that whoever had the authority of the state had *all* of it: decision-making, implementation, and

1.4 Institutions

adjudication. Similarly, what made the absolute monarch of feudal times absolute was that in the final analysis he or she was decision-maker, implementer, and judge. He or she may not have actually exercised this authority in each particular case, choosing instead to delegate implementation or administration to trusted advisors or ministers, and to delegate judgment of disputes to magistrates. Delegation, though, is only a loan or impermanent transfer of power or authority, and this loan or transfer may be revoked at any time. The point is that the monarch could choose at any time, and often did, to exercise all of these powers. Common to classical and feudal times was a notion of unified sovereignty, located in one person or body of persons. This person or body was to retain the final word on all matters.

The alternate idea, which emerges with liberalism, is the notion of a separation of powers, which means placing the state's power to make decisions in a different set of hands from the state's power to implement decisions, and in a different set of hands from the state's power to judge disputes about decisions. In practice this has also meant placing the responsibility for each function not with a person or body of persons, but with an institution, in which individuals exercise that responsibility. It is thus in the modern state that the institutions of the legislature, the executive, and the judiciary come into their own as distinct (but never wholly separate) institutions.

It is also true that however distinct and separate these institutions are (and the United States is usually regarded as the epitome of separated powers), it is rare for any one to have the sole responsibility for a function of government. At most, an institution has primary responsibility for the function but requires the approval or consent of another or other institutions of the state. To indicate this more clearly we need to discuss the actual organization of institutions within a system or type of government. First, though, some general comments about each institution are in order.

1.4.1 LEGISLATURES

A legislature may be described as a body of individuals organized for the purpose of legislating, or making the laws that will be binding on the community. The history of legislatures is interesting and significant. In medieval times, monarchs who wished to mobilize the public to some great purpose (going to war, mounting a Crusade, etc.) would periodically summon representatives

LEGISLATURES

BICAMERAL			UNICAMERAL
BRITAIN [Parliament] House of Lords House of Commons	**CANADA** [Parliament] Senate House of Commons	**AUSTRALIA** [Parliament] Senate House of Representatives	**SWEDEN** Riksdag **NORWAY** Storting
UNITED STATES [Congress] Senate House of Representatives	**JAPAN** [Diet] House of Councillors House of Representatives	**GERMANY** Bundesrat Bundestag	**NEW ZEALAND** House of Representatives **ISRAEL** Knesset
FRANCE Senate National Assembly	**ITALY** Senate Chamber of Deputies	**SWITZERLAND** Council of States National Council	**DENMARK** Folketing
NETHERLANDS First Chamber Second Chamber			

FIGURE 1.2

of the various classes (or "estates") to an assembly, where they would be expected to give their approval to the business the monarch set before them. The usual classes or estates summoned were members of the Church, the aristocracy, and representatives of the townsfolk and free peasantry. Two points are worth noting. One is that the original purpose of such assemblies was to give approval (and thus legitimacy) to decisions that had already been made by the monarch, but that required public compliance in order to be implemented successfully. One of the changes that accompanied the end of feudalism and the beginning of liberal government is the insistence by legislatures upon taking a more direct hand (if not primary responsibility) for making decisions. The second point of significance is that from their earliest beginnings, legislatures were representative, although not democratic. In practice, then, a legislature is an assembly of representatives entrusted with the authority to legislate, and organized for that purpose.

It is also for historical reasons, generally, that many legislatures consist of two chambers, or "houses" of representatives. As noted, the summoning of the estates meant assembling the representatives of different classes, who could hardly be expected to sit and deliberate together. Hence, the distinction in the British legislature between the (House of) Lords, for bishops and nobles, and the (House of) Commons for commoners (townsfolk and free peasants), a distinction that persists today. In most cases, the reason today for continuing to have two chambers, or a **BICAMERAL** legislature is to embody different principles of representation, particularly in federal countries (see below, Chapter 3). Thus in the United States, the House of Representatives is based on the principle of **REPRESENTATION BY POPULATION** (see Chapter 4), while the senate is based on the principle of equal representation of the states. Names of some legislatures, bicameral (two houses) and **UNICAMERAL** (one chamber) are listed in Figure 1.2.

1.4.2 EXECUTIVES

Executives are the highest ranking individuals in organizations; this as true of businesses, or universities, or charities, as it is of nation-states. Modern executive offices within the state are a result of the successive limitation, formalization, or replacement with a civilian counterpart of the traditional office of monarch. As we have noted, absolute monarchs were both makers and administrators of the law; a key accomplishment of the liberal revolution was giving real legislative power to legislatures or parliaments. This has meant that political executives in the modern period have been primarily concerned with what we have identified as the executive (or administrative) function: overseeing the administration or execution of authoritative decisions. This is the day-to-day functioning of government, or what might be called the ongoing activity of governing, and as the size and level of government activity has expanded so enormously in the past two centuries, so, too, the scope of the administrative side of the state has grown in significance, especially given that this includes all of the vast bureaucracies involved in delivering government programs and other public goods.

Before examining the different forms that the modern executive takes, it is necessary to explain a simple but crucial distinction, between *formal* and *discretionary* power or authority. Formal authority is governed by rules, is procedural, and is often exercised in the name of the organization or body by an individual who is its representative. One should not conclude that because formal authority excludes individual discretion or decision that it is unimportant; formality attaches a legitimacy to decisions and this allows others to recognize their validity. For example, when students graduate from university, their diploma is signed by the university president (or equivalent official), and without this signature it would not be a valid diploma. The signature is a formality, however, in that the university president does not personally decide whether or not to sign each student's diploma. Instead, as long as certain rules and procedures have been satisfied (the student has a passing grade in a sufficient number and mix of courses, all outstanding fees have been paid, etc.) the signature of the university president is automatic, *and* informs one and all that this student *has* satisfied the requirements of the university degree. At the level of the nation-state, the **HEAD OF STATE** is the executive whose task it is to perform formal functions on behalf of the state, as well as ceremonial duties, which likewise do not involve great matters of decision, but satisfy certain international and domestic requirements of etiquette. Whether the head of state carries out *only* formal and ceremonial functions will depend on the constitution of the state concerned, but where this is so, the head of state may be referred to as a **FORMAL EXECUTIVE.**

Obviously, not all power, and not all executive acts, are formal. There is a considerable range of executive decisions that involve actual discretion or judgment on the part of those who make them. The fact that there are no rules or procedures executives must follow in these cases is the reason we call this kind of decision-making **DISCRETIONARY POWER** or authority, although it is probably just what we normally think of as what power and authority involve—making decisions. To give just one example that anticipates our discussion below of constitutional systems, consider the difference between law-making in Canada and the U.S. In both these countries, as in many democracies, a bill that passes the legislature goes to the executive for approval. In Canada, this is a mere formality: the governor-general, as a head of state whose role is largely (although not completely) formal, has no choice but to "give assent" to the bill and thus make it law. In the United States, by contrast, the President (who is head of state, but is not a merely formal executive) has several choices, including the option of vetoing (canceling or negating) the legislation; this is the discretionary power a formal executive lacks.

As noted above, modern executives can be explained as various transformations of traditional monarchy. In *constitutional monarchies* (all of which are parliamentary systems, like Canada, Britain, Belgium, Sweden, and others), the role of the monarch has been limited and formalized; what discretionary executive power remains is transferred to a **POLITICAL EXECUTIVE**. This means, first, that unlike the monarch, who usually achieves office by birth and rules of hereditary succession, the political executive is designated by the operations of the political process, which in liberal states is representative and democratic. It also means that these countries have a *dual executive*, consisting of a formal executive (the monarch) and a political executive (usually a **PRIME MINISTER** and **CABINET**).

The historical assumption underlying traditional monarchy (and aristocracy) was that of a natural hierarchy of superior and inferior natures, natures that are at least in part inherited. The Enlightenment liberal view, by contrast, is that all humans are in essence of one common nature, equally deserving of rights and respect. The political community corresponding to this view cannot accept any "natural hierarchy," but is an association of free and equal citizens; a government of free citizens is called a **REPUBLIC**. The logically simplest path to a republic would be to replace the monarchy with a civilian office whose occupant was chosen by the citizen body, i.e., a president. Traditional institutions like monarchy, though, are often deeply imbedded in the political culture and life of a country, so that not only does the monarch resist being deposed, but the monarchy commands fierce loyalty from considerable portions of the public. In practice, to replace a monarch with a presidency has often been difficult, requiring revolution, or conquest and reorganization by a foreign power, or a military coup. Normally, a president will embody the role of head of state and carry out the formal and ceremonial executive functions. In systems with a single executive (like the U.S.), the president will also have responsibilities of a discretionary or political nature. The extent of these will depend, though, on the relationship of the presidency to other institutions like the legislature, and thus depend on the nature of the constitutional system. For the moment, we can consider the president to be the civilian equivalent of a monarch, the extent of his/her power dependent on the place of the presidency within the constitution (see also Figure 1.3, and Chapter 2).

In systems of separated executive-legislative power, a president will be accountable to the people, directly or indirectly. Not all republics are democratic, however, and when authoritarian rulers take the title of president the civilian equivalence of absolute monarchy is achieved. In either case, democratic or authoritarian, we have so far been talking of a strong president, i.e., a unified or single executive. In countries where the monarch's role was diminished and formalized, there emerged a political executive exercising the bulk of discretionary power. This was the experience

EXECUTIVES

UNLIMITED STATES	CONSTITUTIONAL STATES	
AUTHORITARIAN RULER Absolute Monarch	**SINGLE (UNIFIED) EXECUTIVE** Strong President	United States

	DUAL EXECUTIVE
	CONSTITUTIONAL MONARCHY
	    Head of State: Monarch (formal)
	    Head of Government: Prime Minister
	    (political)
		Australia, Belgium, Canada,
		Denmark, Japan, Luxembourg,
		Netherlands, New Zealand,
		Norway, Spain, Sweden,
		United Kingdom

	REPUBLIC (1)
	    Head of State: Weak President (formal)
	    Head of Government: Strong Prime
	    Minister (political)
		Austria, Germany, Greece,
		Iceland, Ireland, Israel, Italy,
		Portugal

	REPUBLIC (2)
	    Head of State: Strong President (political)
	    Head of Government: Prime Minister
	    (political)
		France, Finland, Poland,
		Russia

FIGURE 1.3

of parliamentary systems (to be discussed in greater detail below), where the executive, strictly speaking, is a collective body—the cabinet. In these countries, at the head of the cabinet, and thus the **HEAD OF GOVERNMENT**, is a prime minister. The dual executive in parliamentary systems was initially in most cases a pairing of monarch and prime minister. In some parliamentary countries the monarchy has been replaced with a civilian head of state, normally designated as president. Here, then, is a dual executive of a president who is head of state (a mainly formal office) and a prime minister who is head of government (wielding discretionary power as chair or head of cabinet). As a generalization, the presidency as sole executive is strong; but a presidency as head of state within a dual executive (e.g., in parliamentary systems) is weak. For reasons that will be clearer when we have examined the differences between systems with fused powers (parliamentary) and separated powers (presidential), the most "powerful" executive office in democratic or constitutional regimes is that of prime minister in a parliamentary system.

1.4.3 JUDICIARIES

JUDICIAL INDEPENDENCE

Theodore Becker (1970: 44) has defined judicial independence as

"(a) the degree to which judges believe they can decide and do decide consistent with their own personal attitudes, values, and conceptions of judicial role (in their interpretation of the law),

(b) in opposition to what others, who have or are believed to have political or judicial power, think about or desire in like matters, and

(c) particularly when a decision adverse to the beliefs or desires of those with political or judicial power may bring some retribution on the judges personally or on the power of the courts."

In practical terms, this means that judges must have an adequate salary that is secure from interference by political actors; that their term of office must also be secure, with removal prior to the end of term occurring only for "just cause"; and that the appointment process is free of political pressure or influence.

FIGURE 1.4

The third institution of the state—the judiciary—is in normal cases part of the state, but not part of politics. By judiciary we indicate magistrates or judges and the courts over which they preside. The task of the courts and their officers is the administration of justice, or what we have described as adjudicating disputes about authoritative decisions. A central principle of modern liberal justice (perhaps *the* principle) is the rule of law, which can be summarized as *the requirement that all citizens, rulers and ruled alike, obey known, impartial rules.* In short, no one is above the law, including the highest political officials. For this to be true, and for the law to be impartial, the ideal of **JUDICIAL INDEPENDENCE** must be met. This means that officers of the court, and judges particularly, must be free from political interference, that is, remain free from being influenced by those in positions of authority or power (see Figure 1.4). To the degree that judicial independence is realized in modern democracies, the ordinary business of the courts is a legal, not political, matter.

Two activities of the courts do have unquestionably political significance. One is the interpretation of law, the other is hearing constitutional cases. In applying laws to particular cases, judges are always engaged in interpretation of the law, i.e., clarifying the meaning of the words in the statute, and their relevance to the case at hand. This has political significance when the interpretation judges give a law has unexpected consequences, especially when these are contrary to the intention(s) of lawmakers. Law is an instrument politicians use to make policy; if the courts interpret law in a way different than legislators intended, then judges are making policy—whether they intend to or not. Whether political actors can restore the original policy by making a new, differently worded law depends on a number of legal and political factors.

The most intentionally political role of the courts is to uphold the constitution, the framework of basic law that defines relationships between rulers, institutions, and citizens. If governments are to be limited in their activities by a set of rules such as a constitution provides, then there must be a forum where challenges to actions of the state or government can be heard and authoritative judgments delivered. While many question the need for the courts to make policy, few challenge the legitimacy of the constitutional role of this institution. The scope of this role depends on the nature of the constitution, and on the organization of the courts.

In most countries, courts are organized hierarchically, in a pyramid that culminates in a high court from which there is no further legal appeal. The rulings of this court are binding on all lower courts and this ensures some uniformity to the application and interpretation of the law and, to the degree that uniformity imparts fairness, delivers justice. The high or supreme court is often the final court of appeal for all criminal and civil cases heard at lower levels of the court system. In many countries it also hears constitutional challenges, but in some cases there is a special constitutional court that only deals with this type of case (e.g., Austria, Germany, Italy, Portugal, Spain, France, and most countries of Eastern Europe).

As noted, the actual role of the courts in respect to constitutional matters will depend on several variables. In most cases, the courts will be able to rule on whether government bodies or office-holders have exceeded the authority the constitution allots them. An important but more specialized function relates to disputes between levels of government, a central question in countries with a federal constitution (Chapter 3). Perhaps the most important variable is whether the courts are empowered to perform **JUDICIAL REVIEW**, that is, whether the courts are able to rule on the validity of laws passed by the legislature. The possibility of judicial review is enhanced by the inclusion in the constitution of a code or charter of citizens' rights, because this provides a set of standards that the courts can use to evaluate legislation, but there are several other variables involved in judicial review. "Concrete" review, for example, refers to consideration of a law resulting from an actual case tried under that law. Usually this means that the defendant charged under the law chooses to challenge the constitutional validity of the law. In the U.S., appeal to the Supreme Court of an actual case is the only way judicial review by this body can happen. In Canada, the device of *reference* makes it possible for governments to use the courts to rule on the constitutionality of a bill or law in the absence of an actual case. (Ironically, one reason for doing so is to avoid anticipated court challenges that may bog down application or enforcement of the law.)

REFERENCE is an example of what is called "abstract" review, that is, review in the absence of a case. In some countries, only abstract review is possible; in some countries there is a time limit to the possibility of abstract review after the passage of a bill; and in some countries review *must* take place before a bill actually becomes law. In France, for example, the Constitutional Council may not overturn a bill once the president has signed it into law, so

JUDICIAL REVIEW

DEMOCRACIES WITH JUDICIAL REVIEW:
Australia, Austria, Canada, Denmark, France, Germany, Iceland, Ireland, Italy, Japan, Norway, Sweden, United States

DEMOCRACIES WITHOUT JUDICIAL REVIEW:
Belgium, Finland, Israel, Luxembourg, Netherlands, New Zealand, Switzerland, United Kingdom

[from Lijphart, 1984: 193]

FIGURE 1.5

bills are referred to this special court after passage by the legislature and before presidential assent. Where abstract review is possible, there are usually rules about who can make such a reference to the courts. In some countries, like Sweden, judicial review is constitutionally possible, but rarely happens; in the Netherlands by contrast, judicial review is constitutionally prohibited.

1.5
Systems

As the discussion of institutions makes clear, it is difficult to separate legislatures and executives from the types of political systems in which they are found. By a political (or constitutional) system (or type) we mean to indicate two things: (1) the relationship between the institutions just discussed—legislatures, executives, and judiciaries, and (2) how responsibility for the functions of the state is allocated among these institutions. Fortunately, there is less variety than one might think among the world's democracies. We will outline some of the principles that distinguish the principal varieties, and then in the subsequent two chapters explore these types in greater detail.

One basis of distinction has been the relationship of the institutions of state or, between **CONCENTRATED** and **DISPERSED** powers of government. The parliamentary system of Great Britain epitomizes the former; the presidential system of the U.S. exemplifies the latter. Accordingly, some also refer to this distinction as one between parliamentary and presidential systems. The difficulty with this is that the stable, successful democracies *other* than the United States that have strong presidents are more likely to resemble parliamentary systems than the U.S. constitution. For this reason it is perhaps best to stick to concentrated versus dispersed powers (or fused versus separated), and suggest why the concentration of powers offered by parliamentary systems has proven more durable and attractive, even if, in some cases, it has been supplemented by a strong presidency.

1.5.1 SEPARATED POWERS (PRESIDENTIAL SYSTEMS)

While the British system of parliamentary government was the product of a revolution against absolutist monarchy, the American system of separated powers was in part the result of revolution against the concentrated powers of the British Crown. We say "in part," because revolution in and of itself cannot explain the distrust of government that has been so imbedded in American political culture and the constitution (France, after all, has had several revolutions, and yet has one of the most activist states and political cultures in the democratic world). The framers of the American constitution were also intrigued by the causes of the collapse of the ancient republic of Rome, and worried about the possible rise and dominance of factions within the body politic. They drew heavily on Locke's notion of a clear separation of the executive and legislative powers of the state, and on Montesquieu's ideas about mixed government. To some degree the revolution and the pre-revolutionary experience of the colonials only reinforced the antipathy to government that had brought many of them to the New World in the first place.

While the **PARLIAMENTARY SYSTEM** has evolved from very non-democratic origins (sovereignty embodied in the person of the monarch) to increasingly representative and democratic formations, the U.S. system begins with the liberal notion of popular sovereignty. The people entrust sovereignty to the institutions of the state by means of a constitution, which is their safeguard against abuses of power by those who exercise it. Although it is commonly observed that the constitution framers were wary of government, it is clear that they were pretty hard-headed about the people, too. As James Madison wrote in *Federalist Paper* No. 51: "If men were angels, no government would be necessary. If angels were to govern men, neither external nor internal controls on government would be necessary. In framing a government which is to be administered by men over men, the great difficulty lies in this: you must first enable the government to control the governed; and in the next place oblige it to control itself. A dependence on the people is, no doubt, the primary control on the government; but experience has taught mankind the necessity of auxiliary precautions." In fact, Madison displayed a particularly modern confidence in institutions, in the ability to secure justice through the clever design of institutions and procedures. In several respects, the Constitution is sovereign in the American system of government.

The most fundamental principle of the Constitution is a radical **SEPARATION OF POWERS**. This is accomplished by the creation of distinct "branches" of government and the restriction that no individual may serve or hold office in more than one of these branches at the same time. Thus, unlike the parliamentary convention where members of the cabinet also hold seats in the legislature, the American Constitution requires a member of Congress (the U.S. legislature) to resign that seat if appointed to

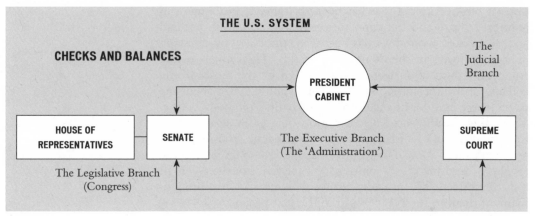

FIGURE 1.6

the cabinet. In Britain, the highest court is actually the House of Lords (the upper chamber of the legislature), although carried out in practice by nine Law Lords (with the right to sit in the House of Lords). In the U.S., the Supreme Court constitutes a third branch of government, balancing the executive branch (President and cabinet) and the legislative branch (Congress: the Senate and House of Representatives).

Auxiliary to the notion of the separation of powers in the American constitution is a set of **CHECKS AND BALANCES** designed to keep any one branch of government from gaining power at the expense of the others. This is one of the "auxiliary precautions" Madison referred to, and is based on the premise that "Ambition must be made to counteract ambition" (*Federalist Paper* No. 51). The actual checks and balances are numerous, but their effect is that no branch of government can fully perform its function without at least the acquiescence of the other two. Thus, while each branch of government has primary responsibility for carrying out the function for which it is named, the other two branches also have a role with respect to that function. The legislature legislates (makes law), but as noted above, the President has the ability to veto legislation, and the Supreme Court by exercising judicial review, can declare laws to be unconstitutional. By the same token, with a two-thirds vote in both houses, Congress can overturn a presidential veto, and through a complex procedure involving the state legislatures, the Constitution can be amended. The president makes high-level appointments, from ambassadors and cabinet secretaries to Supreme Court justices, but the senate of the legislature has the ability to hold hearings on these appointments and in some cases (e.g., Supreme Court appointments) to deny them. And so on.

The third principle that explains this system is the notion of **MIXED GOVERNMENT**, the idea of combining elements of monarchy, aristocracy, and democracy in a constitution, an idea that can be traced back to Aristotle. The executive branch, centered on the President, represents the monarchic element, and provides an example of a single unified executive fulfilling formal, ceremonial, and discretionary executive functions (including ultimate command of the American military). The Supreme Court, a panel of nine justices, represents the aristocratic element of government, although one can see the cabinet and the Senate as somewhat aristocratic in temper, also. Finally, the democratic element is represented by Congress, in particular the House of Representatives, which is elected on the basis of representation by population (the Senate represents the states, each with two senators).

In clear contrast to the parliamentary system, there is no concept of "responsible government" in the U.S. system; indeed, power is so dispersed in the presidential system that one might even say that there is no identifiable government here. It is possible to speak of the Clinton Administration or the Bush Administration, but this refers only to the President, his cabinet, and White House staff members who have no control over the legislature. For a variety of reasons it may be rare for the American cabinet to meet collectively; by and large each Secretary presides individually over a large administrative bureaucracy or set of bureaucracies. Those who make the laws and those who implement them are thus two separate sets of people. Not only may there be little cooperation between the executive and the legislature, there is also no group within the legislature that exercises clear control. In the first place, because there is no responsible government, American political parties have remained weak, relatively undisciplined bodies; the control of party leaders over their legislative members is tenuous at best. Second, unlike many legislatures, the American Congress has two strong chambers, which may often be working at cross-purposes.

In the parliamentary systems, members of the legislature (or at least of the "confidence chamber") *and* thus the members of the cabinet face the electorate at the same time; responsibility for policies, successful, unsuccessful, or lacking, is fairly easy to assign. In the United States constitution, the terms of office are: the President, four years; Congressional representatives, two years; and senators, six years, staggered one-third each two years. Combine these staggered terms with the absence of a unity between legislature and executive and the weakness of party discipline, and the ability to assign responsibility for what does or doesn't happen in U.S. government is dubious. It is not impossible for President, Senate, and House of Representatives to work together, but Madison's intention of setting "ambition against ambition" has worked well enough to ensure that this is as much the exception as the rule.

All of this combines to make the U.S. government, as Madison and the other constitution framers intended, a weak government. This fact is sometimes obscured by the economic and military might of the U.S., particularly as it is now also the world's third most populous nation-state. Nonetheless, relatively speaking, the separation of powers and corresponding checks and balances have put more obstacles in the way of government action than are present in parliamentary systems. This has meant that the enormous growth of the state in the twentieth century in advanced industrial societies was not nearly so large in the U.S. as in most parliamentary countries. While this no doubt has pleased those of a more libertarian frame of mind, it has been partially responsible for several troubling features of current American life—the most unequal distribution of wealth in the industrial world, continued racial inequalities and lack of opportunity, inner-city decay, a crumbling domestic infrastructure, one of the world's highest crime rates—and thwarts the attempts of political actors to address these problems.

When the American executive and legislative branches are able to work together, they must still satisfy the review of their actions performed by the courts. The United States has one of the world's longest and busiest traditions of judicial review, dating back to the celebrated *Marbury vs. Madison* case of 1804. One reason for this is the inclusion in the American constitution of a Bill of Rights, which provides a set of criteria the courts can apply to their review of legislation. Because the American constitution reserves rights to citizens on the one hand, and to the states on the other, the ability of the federal government to act is constrained from the outset. In the 1930s, a conservative Supreme Court over-turned legislation that was central to President Roosevelt's "New Deal" package of measures designed to combat the social and economic effects of the Depression. Roosevelt threatened to try to amend the Constitution in ways that would allow him to change the composition of the court. On the other hand, in the 1950s and 1960s, a liberal Supreme Court made landmark civil rights rulings that signaled the end of racial segregation and led directly to significant civil rights legislation in the Kennedy and Johnson years. Both examples illustrate the importance of the judiciary as a third branch of government in the U.S.

1.5.2 CONCENTRATED POWERS (PARLIAMENTARY SYSTEMS)

The British parliament at Westminster has been called the mother of all parliaments, and indeed most parliamentary constitutions offer variations on the basic arrangements put in place by the Whig Revolution of 1688, itself the product of struggles predating the English Civil War of 1642. The word "revolution" implies a turning upside down, and just such a reversal occurred in the respective roles of the monarch and of the legislature. Prior to 1688, the monarch made decisions (acted) and expected the legislature (particularly the House of Commons) to give formal approval (ratification) to these executive acts. Since 1688, the reverse has been true: the legislature acts and the monarch gives the formal approval (assent) that legitimizes these actions.

This diagram is misleading in two respects. In the first place the shift presented should be understood as one of *relative* influence in government; the British system is one of **PARLIAMENTARY SUPREMACY**, not legislative supremacy. In the British constitution neither the monarch nor the legislature can act alone (legislative supremacy implies the latter) but must act together:

Parliament = The Monarch
+ House Of Lords
+ House Of Commons

Within this whole, the revolution of 1688 reversed the priorities of the players; the play goes on with the same actors, but they have been required to exchange roles.

The second respect in which the characterization is inaccurate is that it leaves out the cabinet (and prime minister) and thus implies more power for the legislative chamber called the House of Commons than is actually the case. As we will see, the cabinet actually exercises discretionary power within parliamentary systems; the cabinet is the government of the day. This cabinet is linked to the legislature in two important ways, but first, we should explain the origin of cabinet government.

While absolute monarchs were ultimately responsible for all activities of the state—as Louis XIV said, "L'Etat c'est moi" (I am the state)—normally they delegated much of the actual labor to trusted advisors. Over time, assistance to the monarch was recognized in a set of offices, each with its own title and particular set of functions (looking after the treasury, or the King's cavalry,

BEFORE 1688

| KING | Acts (discretionary power) |

▼

| HOUSE OF COMMONS | Ratifies (formal power) |

AFTER 1688

| KING | Ratifies (formal power) |

▲

| HOUSE OF COMMONS | Acts (discretionary power) |

FIGURE 1.7

or granting licenses to trade, etc.). Individually, those holding such offices had a title like Minister or Secretary, and collectively they met as advisors to the monarch (in England this body was known as the Privy Council). Originally, the monarch appointed his/her ministers from the ranks of the aristocracy, choosing favorites, and dismissing them once they fell out of favor. This is the origin of the cabinet: a body of officials individually responsible for administering a portion of the state bureaucracy, and collectively forming the "government" of the day. As a body performing the executive function of the state, the cabinet is a **COLLECTIVE EXECUTIVE**.

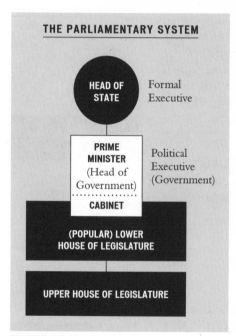

THE PARLIAMENTARY SYSTEM

HEAD OF STATE — Formal Executive

PRIME MINISTER (Head of Government) — Political Executive (Government)

CABINET

(POPULAR) LOWER HOUSE OF LEGISLATURE

UPPER HOUSE OF LEGISLATURE

FIGURE 1.8

The cabinet arose, then, as a body of advisors serving the monarch, with a limited relationship to the legislature. In England, after 1688, this changed in two ways. It was necessary for the monarch to choose his/her ministers from the more powerful chamber of the legislature; as a result of social, economic, and political changes this was no longer the House of Lords (representing the aristocracy), but the House of Commons (representing the propertied interests of an emerging market society). In other words, those who were actually carrying out the executive function (and functioning as a collective executive), were also legislators drawn from the lower chamber of the legislature. This dual membership of cabinet members in both the executive and the legislature is called a **FUSION OF POWERS**, and is common to almost all parliamentary systems.

The second change brought about by 1688 was the requirement that the cabinet (or Ministry, or Privy Council) have the continued support of the most powerful chamber of the legislature—the House of Commons. This is known as "**MAINTAINING THE CONFIDENCE**" of the legislature, and in bicameral parliaments, the lower or popularly representative chamber is the one that matters—is the confidence chamber. Maintaining the confidence means being able to sustain the support of a majority of legislators present in the chamber on all important votes concerning government policy or expenditure. This requirement that the executive (the cabinet) have the support or confidence of the legislature (the lower chamber) is the principle of **RESPONSIBLE GOVERNMENT**, and it is *the* most important feature that distinguishes parliamentary government from all others. The principle intends to keep the executive accountable to the legislature, and in English

important!

politics meant that, instead of pleasing the monarch, the cabinet must be ultimately pleasing to the House of Commons. Any cabinet that fails to maintain the confidence of the legislature is expected to resign, and be replaced by another that is able to command such a majority.

Both the fusion of powers and responsible government in Britain (and many other countries) are **CONVENTIONS**. A convention is an unwritten rule that is nonetheless binding because all parties agree to it (and the reason they agree to it is usually because it works, or works best, to do so). In the case of responsible government, the convention that a government failing to win majority support in the legislature must resign has a clearly practical basis. If the cabinet cannot gain the support of a majority, it cannot get its policies or its expenditures passed, and if it cannot make policy or spend money, it cannot govern.

Linking the political executive—the cabinet—to the legislature by means of responsible government and the fusion of powers has had (at least) two other consequences of note. One is the emergence of the Prime Minister at the top of the political executive, so much so that as head of government the Prime Minister is the most powerful individual in a parliamentary democracy. One popular account has it that the office of Prime Minister emerged to prominence in England in the eighteenth century when German-speaking English kings stopped attending cabinet meetings because of their lack of facility with the English language. Historian Christopher Hill, however, notes that George I "stopped attending the cabinet not because of any lack of linguistic ability but because he had so little authority there" (1969: 216). Since it was now necessary for the cabinet to maintain the support of the House of Commons, monarchs had to choose ministers who could command that support, individuals with great following and influence among the Members of Parliament. Once installed in cabinet, it was these individuals who would determine government policy. Should the King insist on policy contrary to the wishes of the cabinet, he would risk its resignation, the loss of the government, and setting himself at odds with the entire House of Commons. After the Civil War and the Revolution of 1688, English monarchs were reluctant to antagonize Parliament to that extent. Since the eighteenth century in Britain, and now the norm in most parliamentary systems, the Prime Minister (as chair of cabinet and thus head of government) controls most of the discretionary executive authority of the state, and given the fusion of powers that links the cabinet and PM to the House of Commons, usually dominates (if not controls) the legislature's business.

The second development, and one that clinched the dominance of the PM and cabinet within the parliamentary system, was the emergence of strong (disciplined) parties. Students are no doubt fully aware of the central role of political parties within contemporary politics, and we will discuss the nature and functions of political parties in greater depth below. What may be less familiar is the fact that in the early days of representative, parliamentary government, there were no political parties. Individuals stood for parliamentary election on their own merits or reputations, neither representing nor sponsored by some larger organization or association. Within the legislature, it is true, individuals did not act as complete "independents," but associated in factions or groups organized around an ideological disposition, a religious affiliation, personal influence and obligations, naked ambition, or resentment of another group currently in power. Selecting individuals to the cabinet would be in part a calculation of which factions' support they might bring or control and thus contribute to putting together a legislative majority (which responsible government requires). Because the convention of responsible government requires the cabinet to maintain the support of a majority, this provides a great incentive for political leaders to organize their supporters and provide some greater measure of predictability and discipline to their legislative behavior. In parliamentary systems the stakes are high, because failure to maintain a majority means losing office. Consequently, in British parliamentary experience strong parties (now the norm in parliamentary regimes) replaced loose factions. What makes parties strong is their ability to discipline members through rewards for loyal behavior, and sanctions for failure to support the party leadership. As parties have developed, they have come to dominate the political process of democratic states, so much so that being elected to Parliament as an "independent" is now a rather exceptional accomplishment. In many cases, the rules of parliamentary procedure have been revised or re-written to reflect (or ensure) the reality that the primary actors within the system are parties, not individual members.

Strong parties provide structure and predictability to activity within parliament. As organizations that provide means for leaders to discipline members, parliamentary parties are hierarchical and (largely) run from the top down. To some degree, then, although party discipline is a product of the conditions created by responsible government, it also tends to undermine responsible government as

RESPONSIBLE GOVERNMENT AND PARTIES

The division of Parliament (in Britain, Canada, and some other former British colonies) into a government side and an opposition side and the designation of the leader of the largest party not in government as the Leader of Her (His) Majesty's Loyal Opposition are carry overs from the time before disciplined parties. Members of the House would simply declare themselves for or against the government of the day, and take their seats on the appropriate side of the chamber.

FIGURE 1.9

a means by which the legislature keeps the executive accountable. This is so because **PARTY DISCIPLINE** means that party leaders in the cabinet have firm control over the votes of their members in the legislature. The executive dominance described above is thus confirmed and strengthened with the development of strong, disciplined parties. Ultimately, the executive answers not to the legislature, but to the electorate.

This last point is important. Parliamentary government is strong government. The executive is normally a relatively cohesive, collective body that controls both the executive and legislature, and maintains this control through the mechanisms of party discipline. Because of its strength and strategic location within the political system, the cabinet government of a parliamentary system controls not only the legislative process, but also, and more importantly, the making and implementation of public policy. A Prime Minister in such a system can wield as much or more power than any absolute monarch ever enjoyed. One safeguard against the abuse of this power is the ability to appeal to the courts for any violation of the constitution. In many countries, though, there is no judicial review, as we have noted, so constitutional challenges are limited. (In Britain, not only is there no judicial review, there is no written constitution, which is why we have had very little to say about the courts in discussing British parliamentary evolution.) The other, and in the final analysis, most important check against the abuse of power within parliamentary regimes is the power of public opinion, expressed most decisively (although not only here) at election time. This is why democracy requires not only free elections, but a free press, and a sufficiently organized political opposition, an educated citizenry, and as full an access to information about policy decisions as possible.

1.5.3 COMPARING SYSTEMS

As the world embraced democratic regimes in ever greater numbers during successive waves of democratization, a lively debate has emerged over the relative strengths and weakness of concentrating powers in a fused system of executive-legislative relations or separating them. As European colonial empires were being dismantled during the post-1945 era of decolonization, many developing nations inherited parliamentary regimes modeled on their former imperial "mother country." However, America's success with a presidential regime has encouraged American foreign

KEY TERMS

adjudication
amending procedure
bicameral
bureaucracy
cabinet
checks and balances
collective executive
common law
concentrated powers
constitution
constitutionalism
convention
decision-making
discretionary power
dispersed powers
executive
formal executive
functions
fusion of powers
head of government
head of state
implementation
institutions
judiciary
judicial independence
judicial review
legislative
legislation
maintaining confidence
material constitution
mixed government
parliamentary system
parliamentary supremacy
party discipline
policy
polity
political executive
precedent
president
prime minister
reference
representation by population
republic
responsible government
separation of powers
statutes
Supreme Court
unicameral

policy makers to attempt to foster similarly structured regimes in new democracies that were being established abroad. As these new democracies consolidate, we are able to identify some general patterns with respect to the relative merits and faults of these systems as they arise when introduced in non-Western settings. American students may well be surprised at some of the results. We'll turn to a discussion of these in the next chapter, after we've discussed the characteristics and main variations on the two basic forms of regimes.

REFERENCES AND SUGGESTED READING

Bagehot, Walter. 1870. *The English Constitution.* Oxford: Oxford University Press. First published 1867.

Becker, Theodore L. 1970 *Comparative Judicial Politics: The Political Functionings of Courts.* Chicago: Rand McNally.

Bogdanor, Vernon. 1988. *Constitutions in Democratic Politics.* Aldershot, UK: Gower.

Lijphart, Arend. 1984. *Democracies: Patterns of Majoritarian and Consensus Government in Twenty-One Countries.* New Haven: Yale University Press.

——, ed. 1992. *Parliamentary versus Presidential Government.* Oxford: Oxford University Press.

Mahler, Gregory. 1995. *Comparative Politics: An Institutional and Cross-National Approach.* Englewood Cliffs, NJ: Prentice-Hall.

Strong, C.F. 1963. *A History of Modern Political Constitutions.* New York: Capricorn Books.

Zeigler, Harmon. 1990. *The Political Community.* New York: Longman.

TWO | Presidential versus Parliamentary Systems: Executives and Legislatures in Liberal Democracies

The frequent collapse of presidentialist regimes in about 30 Third World countries that have attempted to establish constitutions based on the "separation of powers" suggests that this political formula is seriously flawed. By comparison, only some 13 of over 40 Third World regimes (31 percent) established on parliamentary principles had experienced breakdowns by coup d'état or revolution up to 1985.
— Fred Riggs, 1994: 72

The principles of a free constitution are irrevocably lost, when the legislative power is nominated by the executive.
— Edward Gibbon, *Decline and Fall of the Roman Empire*, ch.3

2.1 Introduction

The preceding chapter has established in broad outline the basic distinction between constitutional democracies that have separated (presidential) or fused (parliamentary) executives and legislatures. As the "third wave" of democratization has swept over the world, creating new democracies where once authoritarian systems existed, a lively debate has emerged over the suitability for export from the advanced industrial world of these different governmental types. Fred Riggs' comment opening this chapter will doubtless surprise many Americans who have been schooled to regard American-style democracy as the "best" system in the world. However, it is the case that the overwhelming majority of the world's successful democracies are parliamentary systems, whether one defines success in material terms or as the absence of authoritarian interruptions (military or civilian dictatorships). Of the world's advanced industrial democracies, only the U.S. (and to some extent France) has a non-parliamentary constitution. As we will see, preferences concerning which kind of governmental system is best will in part reflect different judgments about the desirability of effective governmental intervention.

2.1 Introduction
2.2 Presidentialism Explored
2.3 Parliamentary Systems
    2.3.1 Majoritarian versus Proportionate Systems
    2.3.2 Majority, Minority, and Coalition Government
    2.3.3 Formation and Dissolution of Parliamentary Governments
    2.3.4 The Head of State
    2.3.5 The Political Executive: Prime Minister and Cabinet
    2.3.6 Policy-Making: Executive Dominance
2.4 Presidentialism in Parliamentary Systems: France as a Hybrid
2.5 Conclusion

In this chapter we delve deeper into each type of governing system, examining some of the operating principles that underpin them and that account for the strength or weaknesses of governments. We will outline the basic features of the American model of presidentialism, based on separated executive and legislative branches of government. Because there is relatively greater diversity within the category of parliamentary democracies as a result of the larger number of these regimes in the advanced industrial world (and because these regimes will be less familiar to American students), this chapter will focus more heavily on identifying patterns in parliamentary systems. One distinction we will explore is based on the electoral and party systems, allowing us to discriminate between majoritarian and proportionate parliamentary systems. We conclude the chapter by discussing an example of a hybrid (mixed) parliamentary/presidential system, the French Fifth Republic (1958-present). The Fifth Republic (which Sartori calls "semi-presidential") has a strong directly elected President added to what is otherwise a parliamentary system. Before turning to this mixed system, we will review the basic features of the presidential type of government.

2.2
Presidentialism Explored

Lijphart (1984) identifies **PRESIDENTIALISM** with a political (and not merely formal) executive that is not drawn from the legislature, and is not responsible to the legislature. This is in clear contrast to the parliamentary executive, which is normally both drawn from, and remains responsible to, the legislature. Sartori identifies a system as presidential "if, and only if, the head of state (president) (1) results from popular election, (2) during his or her pre-established tenure cannot be discharged by a parliamentary vote, and (3) heads or otherwise directs the governments that he or she directs" (1994: 84). In democracies, a presidential executive is elected by the people, directly as in France or Finland, or indirectly as in the United States where the device of an electoral college is employed. The "classic" presidential model is the U.S. system of separated powers, where the entire executive has no standing in or responsibility to the legislature.

As we noted in the preceding chapter, the American constitution rests on the principles of republicanism, mixed government, and a separation of powers (employing checks and balances). The latter is the one with which we are most concerned here, because it establishes the independence of the Presidency (and the cabinet) from the legislature, and this in turn has several important implications. The President is not and cannot be a member of the legislature. The same is true of members of the cabinet, who are appointed by the President. American cabinet Secretaries are not responsible to the legislature, collectively or individually, but rather are individually responsible to the President. As a result, there is no body that can be identified (as in parliamentary systems) as the current government or the government of the day. In the United States reference is often made to "the **ADMINISTRATION**" (and more commonly the "Clinton Administration" or the "Bush Administration," etc.), which encompasses the President, cabinet, and White House officials. The task of each secretary is to oversee the administration of his/her government department and advise the President about needs and problems concerning the ability of the public service to deliver policy consistent with the Administration's purposes. This means a role primarily of implementation of policy determined elsewhere: either in the legislature or by presidential aides and advisors. This cabinet is not a collective executive, and for this reason rarely meets as a whole. Given the size of the American state, and in comparison with parliamentary executives, the American cabinet is small: 15 secretaries (after the addition of the Secretary for Homeland Security), the President, Vice-President, and a few cabinet-level executives, such as the head of the CIA and the Ambassador to the United Nations, bring the total to around 20 members.

In some ways the American counterpart to the parliamentary cabinet is as much contained in Executive branch staff as it is in the formal cabinet. White House officials number around 500 individuals and another 1000 or so in the Executive Office of the President, all freshly appointed with each change in President, and hired to provide a range of support and advisory services to the chief executive. The organization and functioning of this bureaucracy is very much at the discretion of the President and will reflect his leadership philosophy and style. In this structure will be found the President's closest policy advisors, and these aides may often wield more influence on public policy than does the cabinet secretary of the relevant department. Because of the separation of powers, the executive has no legislative standing, and can have an impact on legislation only by influencing legislators or appealing to those whose partisan or ideological attachments make them sympathetic to the executive's position. While the President in particular will not have difficulty finding members of Congress to sponsor legislation reflecting the policy aims of the Administration, there is no guarantee of sufficient support to ensure passage. It is frequently the case that different

PARTIES

Political parties are organizations that serve several functions in the political system, and we discuss them in greater detail in Chapter Twelve. America's parties are the oldest in the world, but are less cohesive than many of their counterparts in other countries. A distinction is sometimes made between the **PARLIAMENTARY** (or legislative) **PARTY**, which consists of all elected members of a party and the **PARTY-AT-LARGE**, which also includes constituency officers and citizens who are members of the party. It is often said that after an election the party-at-large often loses control of the parliamentary party, and this is particularly true if the parliamentary party is in government. Another distinction is between **ELECTORAL PARTIES**, which are parties that contest elections by fielding candidates, and **LEGISLATIVE PARTIES**, which are those parties that actually win seats in the legislature. When we talk about a country's party system, we are talking about the number and strength of the legislative parties. Obviously the number of legislative parties cannot be greater than the number of electoral parties, but the reverse is often true.

FIGURE 2.1

parties control the legislative and executive branches (15 of the past 23 midterm and presidential year elections have resulted in "divided government"), and even where there is a party congruence between the White House and the Congress, the weakness of party discipline means there are no safe bets. While observers have noted a strengthening of party voting (a situation in which a majority of Democrats oppose a majority of Republicans, or vice versa, on legislation) is becoming more common in recent years, the situation is still a far cry from the virtual unanimity of party control over legislative voting that exists in many parliamentary regimes. On the other hand, the defeat of any bill or measure in the legislature is simply that; there is no question of confidence, or of the consequences associated with the lack of confidence, in parliamentary regimes. Parties are weak in part because there is no requirement of responsible government, which works in parliamentary systems as a powerful incentive to create mechanisms of discipline. The weakness of parties means that party labels provide no infallible guide to the voting behavior of legislators: Democrats may vote against legislation sponsored by a Democratic President or supported by the party leadership. Republicans in one chamber might fall overwhelmingly behind a bill, but block its passage in the other house of Congress. The 2002 elections gave the Republicans control of both houses of Congress as well as the White House. But this is certainly no guarantee of success in passing legislation; in addition to the difficulty of enforcing party discipline, in the Senate they will face rules of debate that allow a senator to control the floor in a filibuster that can be ended only by a vote of 60 senators. Compromise will still be necessary.

In the same sense that there is no readily identifiable "government" in this model, there is no head of government. The President is chief administrator and the head of state, performing both formal and political functions, the latter including foreign policy, defense, and considerable emergency powers. It is these latter powers, combined with the relative size and might of the American military on the world stage, that give the U.S. President such prominence internationally. On the other hand, the lack of control over the legislature can mean much less domestic power than a Prime Minister wields in a parliamentary system. An outside observer might well conclude that the willingness of the United States to employ military solutions to problems abroad (e.g., Grenada, Panama, the Persian Gulf, etc.) has nothing to do with innate belligerence, and everything to do with the fact that this is one area where the President can exercise power relatively unhindered by Congress or the Courts.

In contrast to the relative coherence or concentration of authority within parliamentary systems, the separation of powers in the American case creates what its critics describe as a fragmented government, and in many cases, a weak government. Its supporters, on the other hand, celebrate the American system as the epitome of **PLURALIST DEMOCRACY**. Whereas majoritarian parliamentary systems manufacture majorities, and proportionate systems put together a more legitimate consensus through coalition; in either case power is exercised in the period between elections by a fairly static majority. Those not in government, the minority, are left in most cases with very little voice in the policy-making process, and thus with ineffective representation. At its worst, this can become a tyranny of the majority over the minority. The designers of the American constitution wished to avoid just this domination of a minority (they feared that men of property and substance would be submerged in the democratic mass) and so fragmented power through the checks and balances of separated powers. As the term "pluralist" implies, power is centered nowhere within the American state, but is dispersed among various institutions, and diluted by being placed in many hands. As critics point out, the fragmentation of public power may in fact enhance the concentration of private power, and puts no barrier in the way of those with power, money and influence in civil society from coming to have a disproportionate share of influence in all three branches of government (see Parenti, 1978, 1980).

One means by which political power is fragmented, and at the same time a means of balancing the executive and legislative branches of government, is the device of fixed, staggered elections. This balances the branches in that neither has the power to dismiss the other and call an election (in most parliamentary systems the executive can dissolve the legislature and seek early elections, and in Austria the legislature can dissolve itself). Members of the first chamber of Congress (the House of Representatives) serve a two-year term, and Senators (members of the second chamber) serve a six-year term, with one-third of the seats contested every two years. The Presidential term of office is four years, and no President may serve more than two terms. Thus, a Congress elected at the same time as the President may change radically halfway through his term, and a President re-elected may find that many of his congressional allies have gone down to defeat. In fact, it is normal for the President's party to lose seats in the midterm Congressional elections. This was dramatically the case in 1994, when the Democrats not only lost 52 House and eight Senate seats, but also lost majority status in both houses for the first time in four decades. As a result of this, although the 103rd Congress, elected along with President Clinton in 1992, had been dominated by the President's agenda on deficit reduction, economic stimulation, gays in the military, and health care reform, the 104th Congress was dominated by the resurgent Republican Party's "Contract With America." On the other hand, the Republicans proved the exception to this general rule in the 2002 mid-terms by gaining seats in both houses. Although the number of seats changing hands was small, it was enough to allow them to regain control of the Senate. It remains to be seen whether this represents a long-term shift in favor of the Republicans or is, like the 2000 presidential elections, a sign of a very closely divided electorate.

The presence of fixed terms of office removes some potential uncertainty that turns up in parliamentary systems, however. There is, on the other hand, no government formation process, nor are there any of the difficult procedural or constitutional questions about dissolution or defeat of government that arise in parliamentary situations. The business of government tends to be conducted within the constraints provided by the fixed electoral terms and the corresponding congressional calendar, providing considerable predictability to the conduct of public affairs over an administration's term of office.

Another institutional means of fragmenting power in the American system is found in the division of legislative power across two co-equal chambers of houses. Because all legislation must secure majorities in both houses if it is to be forwarded to the president, this system is referred to as one of **STRONG** or **SYMMETRICAL BICAMERALISM**. The House of Representatives, the lower house in this system, is comprised of 435 members, each elected from single-member districts according to the principle of representation by population (with at least one Member for each state). Senators, however, are elected to represent the states in the federal policy process. Each state returns two senators, regardless of the size of the state (and in the 105th Congress 54 senators, a sufficient number to pass legislation, came from states comprising only 20 per cent of the population of the country). While coequals in the legislative process, the two houses are not identical, however. All revenue bills, for example, must originate in the House of Representatives. While the House can bring impeachment charges against a President, only the Senate can try the case. The Senate can scrutinize high-level executive and judicial appointments, therefore, Presidents worry about instances when the Senate is not controlled by the President's party (making the June 2001 defection of Senator Jim Jeffords of Vermont from the Republicans to sit as an independent, thus tipping the balance in the Senate in the Democrats favor, all the more dramatic). To the outside observer, one of the most striking characteristics of the fragmentation of powers in the American system is the elusiveness of public policy, elusive in three ways. First of all, it may simply not be possible to effect public policy, because political actors with conflicting policy preferences are able to thwart each other using the checks and vetoes built into the system. Policy proposed by the President may not be able to marshal enough support in one or both houses of Congress. Legislation passed by Congress may fall to a Presidential **VETO**. Presidents can veto legislation by sending it back to Congress with an explanation of the reasons for rejecting it. In this case, the veto can only be overridden by Congress if the bill is passed again by two-thirds majorities of both the Senate and the House. Only about 4 per cent of all vetoed legislation is able to clear this hurdle. In addition, a President can exercise a **POCKET VETO** whenever Congress adjourns within 10 days of passing a bill. In this event, the President can simply refuse to sign the bill into law and by doing nothing simply let the bill die.

A little passive agressive?

Legislation that passes may be implemented or administered by an indifferent or hostile executive in ways that thwart the legislators' intentions. This is often made possible by the vagueness and lack of detail in the legislation the Congress and the President pass. Often, the details necessary for the implementation of legislation are left to bureaucratic agencies to fill in, on the grounds that the level of technical expertise needed to make these decisions is most often found there.

Second, public policy is elusive because in order to secure passage through so many possible veto points, a series of compromises and trade-offs is often necessary, diluting the effect or changing the outcomes of policy along the way. In recent Congresses, more than 9,000-11,000 bills have been submitted by members every two years (up from 144 bills introduced in the 1st Congress). Only a small percentage survive to become laws, however, and those that make it through this process often bear little resemblance to their initial drafts. To do so, the bills must pass both in the House and the Senate, after which any differences that result from amendments in either chamber are worked out by a conference committee (and subsequently approved by each house), before they can go for Presidential approval. At any point along this path, a failure to act is sufficient to kill a piece of legislation. The need to compromise and build coalitions along this tortuous road inevitably blunts the edge of legislation and dilutes its ideological content. Astute legislators can often attach "riders" to bills in return for their support. These amendments often have nothing to do with the topic of the bill itself.

Third, public policy is elusive in the sense that it is often difficult for citizens to know whom properly to credit for policy successes or to determine who should shoulder the blame for policy failures. There will be no shortage of actors claiming to have played the crucial role in a popular policy, and no shortage of finger-pointing among political actors when there is dissatisfaction with government's performance. This elusiveness of public policy, in all three senses, may well contribute to the large-scale public dissatisfaction with government and with politicians, and account in part for the low turnouts of voters in American elections. Ironically, in a testament to the strength of the American political culture, and the effectiveness of the socialization process, Americans appear to revere their constitution when it may be exactly this constitutional system that leads them to distrust their government and their political classes.

2.3 Parliamentary Systems

At its most basic, the essence of parliamentary government is the relationship between the executive and the legislature, something expressed most succinctly as *responsible cabinet government achieved through a fusion of powers.* This means several things. First, the government in power consists of a cabinet, which is a committee of individuals exercising executive power. Exercising executive power means in turn that each of these cabinet members (usually called ministers) is the executive or head of a government department or set of related departments. The area of responsibility of a cabinet minister is known as a **PORTFOLIO**. Second, the cabinet ministers are drawn from the ranks of the legislature, to which, as a body, they remain collectively responsible. (Exceptions to the parliamentary membership of cabinet ministers are Norway, Netherlands, and Luxembourg, where cabinet ministers do not have a seat in the legislature, although they do participate in parliamentary debates.) While ministers answer individually to the legislature for their portfolio, collectively, the cabinet must retain the support (confidence) of a majority in the legislature. Failure to do so means the end of this particular cabinet and thus the defeat of the government. Although each minister has a particular portfolio, government policy for any and all portfolios is approved by the cabinet, and must have the public support of all members of cabinet. This is known as the principle of **CABINET SOLIDARITY** or of **COLLECTIVE RESPONSIBILITY**, and indicates most clearly that this is a collective executive.

The head or chair of the cabinet is the Prime Minister, sometimes misleadingly described as a "first among equals," misleadingly, because the Prime Minister is usually pre-eminent among ministers, and in many parliamentary systems determines everything that matters about the cabinet, from its size to its membership to its structure to its style of decision-making. As head of cabinet, the PM is thus head of government, and the chief political executive in most parliamentary systems (examples where this is not true will be discussed in the next chapter). Parliamentary systems thus have a dual executive, for someone *other* than the PM will occupy the position of head of state, a formal executive with largely formal and ceremonial functions. Whatever the title of the head of state—king, queen, president, grand duke—it is the Prime Minister as head of government who exercises most of the authority of the state in a parliamentary system.

Finally, parliamentary government is about a **PARTY SYSTEM** of politics. The fusion of powers and the requirements of responsible government provide an irresistible incentive for political parties to become highly structured, disciplined bodies. What we are largely talking about here is the behavior of members of the party who sit in the legislature, or what is usually called the **PARLIAMENTARY PARTY** (or sometimes "caucus"). It is possible for parties to develop mechanisms or procedures for punishing disloyalty within the caucus, and the parliamentary system provides many opportunities for parties to reward loyalty, culminating in cabinet participation. Strong, unified parties, and the competition between them are key ingredients to what happens in the legislature, in the cabinet, and in the relations between cabinet and legislature in normal parliamentary systems. Since the Prime Minister is also the head of his or her party, in addition to being head of government, he or she has a particularly central position within the parliamentary system. It is also here, though, with the relationship of the Prime Minister to the cabinet, and of the cabinet to the legislature, and of cabinet, legislature, and Prime Minister to the political parties, that the distinction alluded to above, between majoritarian and proportionate systems becomes too important to ignore.

2.3.1 MAJORITARIAN VERSUS PROPORTIONATE SYSTEMS

Because parties are so central to parliamentary systems, it makes a real difference to these systems how many parties there are in the legislature, what their relative strength is, and how accurately their representation in the legislature mirrors their support in the electorate. In other words, a fundamental difference between parliamentary systems is the nature of their **PARTY SYSTEM**, and the party system is largely a function of (or associated with) the **ELECTORAL SYSTEM**.[1] Both of these systems will be explained and discussed in greater detail in Chapter 4, and students may wish to skip ahead and skim portions of that chapter before continuing here. Differences related to parties and electoral systems are absolutely crucial for determining how strong or weak, in the sense of being able to pass its preferred legislation, will be the government of a parliamentary system. For this reason, a brief overview of these factors, as they affect government formation and survival in parliamentary systems, is in order.

In terms of electoral systems, we want to distinguish between **PLURALITY** systems, where the candidate with the most votes is declared the winner (as in Canada, the U.S., and Britain), and **PROPORTIONATE REPRESENTATION** systems, where candidates from parties are awarded seats on the basis of the vote for the party. The plurality system is sometimes called a "winner-take-all" system, because the margin of victory makes no difference to the outcome; if I finish with 9,999 votes and you have 10,000, you win the seat and I have nothing to show for second place. The same result happens if I finish with 1 vote and you have 19,999. The plurality system is not good at reflecting the amount of support that winners receive, and this is not only true on a constituency by constituency basis, but also as a whole when the results are aggregated for all electoral districts. As a general rule, and this becomes more likely the more parties there are contesting the election, plurality systems *overcompensate winners* and *penalize losers* (see Figure 2.2).

For a variety of reasons (see Chapter 4), the plurality system has two tendencies with which we are concerned here. One is to deliver a parliamentary majority to the winner of the election, i.e., to ensure that one party wins more seats in the legislature than all other parties combined. Given the tendency of plurality electoral systems to be associated with two-party systems this observation may seem trivial, but it is true also of countries like Canada with many electoral parties. The second tendency is that there is no

1. In some cases, it is clear that the party system led to a proportionate electoral system being adopted, but it is this type of system that reinforces a multi-party system and ensures a high degree of proportionality among parties.

DISPROPORTIONALITY AND CANADA'S ELECTORAL SYSTEM

1867			2000		
PARTY	**SEATS %**	**VOTE %**	**PARTY**	**SEATS %**	**VOTE %**
Conservatives	60	50.1	Liberals	57.1	40.8
Liberals	40	49.9	Canadian Alliance (Reform)	21.9	25.5
			Bloc Québécois	12.6	10.7
			Conservatives	4	12.2
			NDP	4.3	8.5

FIGURE 2.2

necessary correspondence between a party's parliamentary strength and its electoral strength; as a general rule winning parties will receive a higher share of seats in the legislature than their share of vote would warrant, and other parties will be correspondingly penalized by the system. In this way, the parliamentary majority of the winning party is often **MANUFACTURED**, meaning that the party won a majority of seats but received less than a majority of the vote. Figure 2.2 illustrates these tendencies at work in Canada in 1867 and 2000, though similar examples may be taken from Britain or other countries with plurality systems. The tendencies we have associated with plurality systems here are even more likely when the number of parties increases.

Proportional representation electoral systems do not produce these electoral system consequences. The close correspondence between share of parliamentary seats and share of electoral vote has two consequences of note. One is the tendency to sustain a multi-party system, and the significance of this will be more apparent as we proceed. The other is the virtual impossibility of manufacturing a majority. Since the system does not over-reward or penalize parties, the only legislative majorities that result will be fully earned, that is, reflective of a majority of the votes cast by the electorate. The greater the number of electoral parties, the less the likelihood that one will command an absolute majority of support, and since proportionate systems sustain multi-party environments, legislative majorities for a single party are rare in these systems.

Hence, the distinction we are making between majoritarian and proportionate parliamentary systems may be explained as follows:

ELECTORAL SYSTEM		PARTY SYSTEM		TYPE OF PARLIAMENTARY SYSTEM
plurality	+	two-party	=	majoritarian
proportionate	+	multi-party	=	proportionate

By a **MAJORITARIAN SYSTEM** we mean one where the electoral and party system create a general tendency or normal expectation that following an election, one party will have control of a majority of seats in the legislature. By a proportionate system we mean one where the electoral and party system create the conditions where following an election, each party will have a share of seats corresponding to its share of vote, and for one party to control a majority of seats in the legislature will be the exception rather than the rule. A couple of clarifications are in order.

It should be emphasized that we are speaking of general tendencies here, not absolute relations; for every generalization we make there are (or could conceivably be) exceptions. Not all plurality electoral systems produce two-party systems (as the Canadian illustration in Figure 2.2 has clearly demonstrated), but on the other hand the persistence of a multi-party system in a plurality electoral system creates pressures for electoral reform. It is safe to say that plurality systems tend to reflect and sustain two-party environments, and that proportionate systems tend to reflect and sustain multi-party environments, but there are counterexamples to each generalization. Similarly, while it is not impossible for a party to win an absolute majority in a proportionate system with a multi-party environment, so, too, there is no guarantee that a plurality system will always produce a legislative majority for the winning party. What we are concerned with here is the usual or normal outcome of the system, because this will govern the expectations and calculations of the political actors, and create the conventions and norms of institutional behavior within these systems.

If the majority of the world's democracies are parliamentary, then we should also note that of the 22 parliamentary systems that have been continuously democratic since 1945, 15 (Germany, Italy, Sweden, Norway, Denmark, Finland, Iceland, The Netherlands, Belgium, Luxembourg, Ireland, Austria, Switzerland, Malta, and Israel) fit our classification as proportionate; three (the United Kingdom, Canada, and India) are majoritarian; and two (France and Australia) represent special cases, in part because they have neither (single member) plurality nor proportionate representation electoral systems (see Lijphart, 1994: 2). Of these latter two, France has been more like proportionate systems, and Australia more like majoritarian systems. Three European countries that became democratic in the mid-1970s—Greece, Portugal, and Spain—are also proportionate, as are most (if not all) of the newly created democracies of Eastern Europe and the former Soviet Union.[2] Finally, constitutional changes have meant that the most recent elections

2. The youth of these newly democratic regimes makes it premature to regard them as more than proto-democracies at this point in time.

(both 1996) contested in Japan and New Zealand took place for the first time in a proportionate electoral system. The number (and share) of the world's majoritarian parliamentary systems seems to be declining, and may eventually become as anomalous as the American separation of powers constitutional model. However, as the division of countries above indicates, the majority of the world's English-speaking peoples live in non-proportionate systems (parliamentary or otherwise), so we will continue to contrast parliamentary government in majoritarian and proportionate systems in the remainder of this chapter.[3]

2.3.2 MAJORITY, MINORITY, AND COALITION GOVERNMENT

The first set of differences we can note concerns the nature of government in these two types of parliamentary system. If majoritarian systems tend to produce control of the legislature by one party, through a majority that often is manufactured, then obviously the government (cabinet) in such systems will normally be drawn from the caucus of the winning (majority) party. This is what is known as a **MAJORITY GOVERNMENT**, and what should more precisely be called single-party majority government. In other words, the cabinet is drawn from one party, which happens also to have a majority of the seats in the legislature (or in the house of the legislature that serves as the confidence chamber). Given strong party discipline, the requirements of responsible government (i.e., that the cabinet retain the support of a legislative majority) are more or less automatically fulfilled, and one expects single-party majority governments to be very stable. This circumstance also provides for the strongest possible form of government, since a majority of legislators necessary to pass legislation are subject to the discipline of the governing caucus (and a Prime Minister). This situation leads critics of parliamentary systems to describe the Prime Minister as an "elected dictator." Although majority government is possible under any legislative system currently in use, it is much more likely in countries with plurality electoral systems, and less likely where there is proportionate representation.

Suppose, though, that no one party wins a majority of seats in the legislature; who will govern? If the cabinet continues to be drawn from the members of one party in the legislature, this will constitute a **MINORITY GOVERNMENT**, because the government controls (through party discipline) the votes of only a minority of

3. Lijphart (1984) has made an influential distinction between "majoritarian" and "consensual" democracies based on nine variables, only some of which have reference to the parliamentary characteristics we are interested in here. Among other things Lijphart includes are characteristics linked to federalism, and the degree of pluralism within the population of the polity.

members of the legislature. One might expect that the party that forms the government in this situation will be the largest of the parliamentary parties, but this is not necessarily the case, as we will see.

Meeting the requirements of responsible government will clearly be more of a challenge for minority governments; a legislative majority for the government will require the co-operation, active or passive, of at least one other party in the legislature. The general expectation might be, then, that minority governments will be less stable and less strong than single-party majority governments because the possibility at least exists for defeat of the government in the legislature. The stability of minority governments depends on some other factors, foremost being the type of parliamentary system, a point we will explain below.

The other possibility, if no one party controls a legislative majority, is to draw the cabinet from two or more parties that *between them* do control a majority of legislators. This is what is known as **COALITION GOVERNMENT**, which typically means a formal agreement between political parties indicating three things: (1) an agreement jointly to form a government, (2) a division of the cabinet seats between the parties and the allocation of specific portfolios, including that of Prime Minister, and (3) an agreement about policies that the government will implement, or positions it will take on key issues. In many countries, coalition governments are the norm, and in others they arise occasionally. For example, a recent study of 13 Western European governments that experienced coalition governments between 1945 and 1999 (Belgium, Denmark, Finland, France, Germany, Ireland, Italy, Luxembourg, the Netherlands, Norway, Portugal, Sweden, and the United Kingdom) found that coalitions comprised fully 69 per cent of all cabinets formed over that period (Müller and Strøm, 2000).

Strictly speaking, this is what is known as an **EXECUTIVE COALITION**, because the members of the two or more parties share the posts of government (cabinet ministries). Normally, the division of seats between the parties reflects their relative strength in the legislature; if party A contributes twice as many members to the joint legislative majority as party B, then we also can expect party A to hold twice as many seats in cabinet as party B. This norm of proportionality is followed quite faithfully in countries with coalition government. The allocation of portfolios is less predictable, although there are certain affinities between party ideology and favorite cabinet ministries. These decisions, as well as the formal policy agreements, are the result of sometimes intense and protracted negotiations between the parties involved. Although it is possible for coalition governments to control less than a majority of seats in the legislature, this is very unusual, and coalition government is normally an example of multi-party majority government. Unless we state otherwise, this is what we will mean by the term coalition government.

It is also possible in a parliament where no one party controls a majority, for a single-party cabinet to govern with the support of another or other parties in the legislature. Where parties agree to support each other on legislative votes, we have a **LEGISLATIVE COALITION**. Now obviously, any single-party minority government that survives does so on the basis of legislative coalitions. This may be a formal agreement of mutual legislative support, it may be informal but ongoing because of ideological affinity, or it may be a series of shifting legislative alliances. The Swedish Social Democratic Party has governed successfully on many occasions with a single-party minority cabinet because it could count on the support of a small Communist party that could not bring itself to vote with the government's right-wing opposition.

In many European democracies, parties in the center of the system have been able to provide effective minority government by crafting policies that were attractive to opponents on the left some of the time, to opponents on the right some of the time, but never offensive to both right and left together. This is an example of how the type of parliamentary system can make a big difference to the stability of minority governments.

Consider parliaments in countries where the norm is for the electoral system to produce a clear winner, a party controlling a majority of seats in the legislature. A situation where no one party controls a majority of legislators—the precondition of minority government—will be regarded as an abnormality, as an exception to the rule. The expectation will be that the next election will set things right by restoring a single-party majority. Minority government, when it occurs, will be regarded as an unusual or abnormal situation that will be put up with only until enough parties are willing to gamble that their positions will be improved by another election. This describes the position of minority government in most countries with plurality electoral systems, what we have called majoritarian parliamentary systems. (Since plurality electoral systems are more volatile—there is a greater likelihood of significant change in support for any one party from one election to another—than proportionate systems, the gamble that minority government will not simply be repeated is reasonable.)

COALITIONS

EXECUTIVE COALITION

Where two or more parties formally agree to govern, dividing the cabinet posts between them, and (usually) agreeing on a joint policy platform.

LEGISLATIVE COALITION

Where two or more parties agree to vote together in the legislature, but do not share the executive between them.

ELECTORAL COALITION

Where two (or more) parties agree to work together in an election, usually agreeing not to run candidates in the same constituencies, provide mutual support, etc. Implicit in such electoral alliances is the possibility of working together in legislative or executive coalitions.

FIGURE 2.3

SYSTEM / GOVERNMENT	MAJORITARIAN	PROPORTIONATE
Single Party / Majority	the norm	abnormal
Single Party / Minority	abnormal	common
Executive Coalition	exceptional	the norm

FIGURE 2.4

In countries where the norm is for the electoral system to produce no clear winner, where no one party controls the legislature, the expectation will be that some sort of coalition will be formed. In some countries, the size and or the strategic position of the largest party may make a minority government resting on legislative coalitions as attractive or feasible as forming an executive coalition. In countries with proportionate representation electoral systems, with what we have called proportionate parliaments, minority government will be more likely, and will more likely be regarded not as a temporary expedient but a case of "normal politics." Our observations about majority, minority, and coalition government in the two types of parliamentary systems are summarized in Figure 2.4. As we noted above, while it is possible for any of these types of government to be formed in either of the types of parliamentary system, there is in either system a "normal" type of government and an "abnormal" type, abnormal because it works contrary to the tendencies of the electoral and party systems. In addition, we note that minority government may not be the norm, but is extremely common in proportionate systems. Coalition government in majoritarian systems is not simply abnormal, but usually happens under extraordinary circumstances like the state of national emergency associated with war.

2.3.3 FORMATION AND DISSOLUTION OF PARLIAMENTARY GOVERNMENTS

The distinctions we have been discussing have a bearing on two very fundamental aspects of parliamentary government; how it comes into being and how it is dissolved. In the constitution of every parliamentary country a government formation process is outlined, explicitly or implicitly. Contrary to popular perception, and to the way politics is reported in the media, parliamentary governments are not selected by the people, but by the legislature. Elections in parliamentary countries return a set of representatives to the legislature; then the government formation process begins, and it can be simple, or complex. Simple, complex, or in between, government formation in the parliamentary system involves variations on the following basic procedure: (1) the head of state invites someone from the legislature to form and head (as PM) a government, (2) the Prime Minister designate presents a cabinet to the head of state and they are sworn in as ministers of the state, of the Crown, or whatever is appropriate, and (3) the new cabinet government meets the legislature and receives its confidence (or does not).

In majoritarian systems, in the normal course of things, the government formation process is extremely simple: the leader of the party that won a majority of seats in the legislature is invited to form a government. Given strong party discipline, this party will control the legislature, and only a government from this party will receive the confidence of the legislature: there is no one else to ask. The same applies to those rare cases of a single-party majority being returned to the legislature in a proportionate system. If, on the other hand, in either system, no one party receives a majority of seats in the legislature, the process becomes more complicated, and the role of the head of state may be less of a formality. (It is noteworthy that in majoritarian systems, the rules and procedures of the government formation process are much less formal and more likely to be contained in conventions. One is tempted to attribute this to the expectation in these systems that there will be a majority returned to Parliament and that there will be no need of rules to guide the process. On the other hand, most majoritarian systems are copies of the British parliamentary system that has a largely conventional, unwritten constitution.)

When no party commands a majority, there are two logical choices of whom to invite to form the government: (1) the leader of the largest party in the legislature, and (2) the leader of the party that formed or led the previous government.[4] This may be a matter of judgment for the head of state, it may be that there are established conventions about how this decision ought to be taken, or there may be explicit rules in the constitution that instruct the head of state on how to proceed. In European proportional systems, the individual invited to form a government is often called a **FORMATEUR**.

Once a *formateur* has been designated, he/she must decide whether the conditions exist to govern as a single-party minority, or whether it is more prudent to share power with another party or parties. There are advantages either way. A minority means not having to surrender portfolios or commit to a formal policy agreement, but it also means risking defeat in the legislature at any time, and/or making policy compromises on issues to avoid this fate.

4. Consider the situation where there is a "pariah" party—one that no other party will co-operate with, like the situation of the Communists in post-war Italy. Even if this party finishes first, to invite it to form the government is futile because no other party will vote with it. Suppose also that the party that led the previous government has finished fourth in a five-party parliament. In this case, the second place party may be the best placed to lead a government.

TERMINATION OF PARLIAMENTARY GOVERNMENTS

1. **CHANGE IN THE PARTY COMPOSITION OF THE CABINET**
   (a) following internal dissension between coalition partners
   (b) following defeat in the legislature
   (c) following constitutional intervention (executive dismissal —see discussion of France)

2. **A FORMAL GOVERNMENT RESIGNATION**, which may come about for any of the reasons listed in 1 and lead to a new government, but not necessarily involve a change in the party composition of the cabinet.

3. **A CHANGE IN THE PRIME MINISTER:**
   (a) forced retirement (through cabinet or party revolt)
   (b) voluntary retirement
   (c) for health reasons

4. **AN ELECTION,** which may be "forced" by any of the preceding events, but which may also
   (a) be anticipated by a governing party choosing to maximize its electoral chances at a particular moment, or
   (b) be required because of constitutional limitations on the life of Parliament, or because of fixed election dates.

FIGURE 2.5

Coalition government brings stability and predictability at the cost of sharing power and making policy compromises. The decision whether or not to seek partners will depend in the final analysis on the balance of circumstances, and on the expectations generated by the parliamentary system. In majoritarian systems, because the absence of a majority is seen to be a (temporary) aberration, and because coalition is not common, leaders will likely prefer to govern as a minority, expecting to improve their fortunes through an election at the earliest convenient opportunity. In proportionate systems, where coalition is the norm, *formateurs* are likely to seek partners unless conditions for a long-term viable minority government clearly are present.

Curiously, what constitutes the end of government is one of the areas of parliamentary theory on which there is considerable disagreement. Figure 2.5 lists (following Budge and Keman, 1990 and Laver and Schepsle, 1996) four main causes of a termination of (or change in) government, and possible variations in underlying circumstances. Some authors (Lijphart, 1984) regard only a change in the party membership of cabinet (1) to indicate a change in government, so that a mere change in Prime Minister, or an election that doesn't change the party or parties in power doesn't count. Laver and Schofield (1990) regard reasons (1) and (4) as valid terminations of government, but not (2) and (3) if they lead to no difference in the cabinet players. One reason this matters is that a perennial research question in parliamentary politics concerns which form of government is more stable (i.e., lasts longer): majority, coalition (in its various types), or minority? Obviously, the way one defines the termination of government will make a difference in one's findings on stability. This text will treat all four reasons as valid criteria for regarding a government as terminated.

The end of a government means that it must be replaced by another. This means either that the new government will be drawn from the legislature as it stands, or, that there will be an election to return a new legislature, and out of it, a new government. When it is not possible to form a new government out of the existing party standings in the legislature, the head of state may agree to dissolve parliament—what is called **DISSOLUTION**—and issue a call for an election. As we will see, several variables are relevant here, and there are exceptions to every rule.

Moreover, there is *always* a government in power. The termination of a government (almost always) results in the presentation of a formal resignation of the government (or of the Prime Minister) to the head of state. Nonetheless, the government that is being terminated will in fact remain in power until another is instituted to take its place, and until this happens will function as a **CARE-TAKER GOVERNMENT**. This means that the government will continue to administer existing policies and programs but will not introduce new policies or significant legislation. This is only fitting, since the government has either lost the confidence of the legislature, or has voluntarily resigned it. If the existing government has collapsed completely (more likely in a coalition government than otherwise) it may not be able to continue in a caretaker mode. Here the head of state may invite another party or coalition of parties to serve as a caretaker government until new elections or negotiations leading to a viable government can be held.

Consider a single-party majority government, which will most likely be found in a majoritarian system. A change in the party composition of the cabinet is unlikely to happen here *except* through defeat in an election. The odds of a single-party majority government losing the confidence of the legislature and being forced to resign are slim also. It is possible that a government with a very slim majority could become a minority through attrition (as happened to the Conservative government of John Major in the United Kingdom by 1997), and if the majority is razor thin there is always the possibility of a miscalculation in the legislature and of defeat if there should be more government members absent than opposition members. These, though, are exceptions and the normal end of a single-party majority government comes when the government chooses, or because it reaches the end of its term.

In some countries, election dates are fixed (e.g., in Germany and Norway every four years, in Sweden every three years) and the defeat or resignation of a government in the period between necessitates the installation of another government to finish out the time until the election is scheduled. In some cases, election dates are fixed, but there is a provision allowing the head of state to call early elections if there is no possibility of forming a viable government from the parties as currently situated in the legislature. If early dissolution of the legislature and elections are not constitutionally permitted, this is a case where a caretaker government may be necessary to serve the remainder of the period before mandated elections. To our knowledge, fixed electoral terms in the parliamentary world occur only in proportionate systems.

In countries without fixed election dates, the term of government is *flexible* with a maximum time between elections established by the constitution. In most cases, this maximum term is four or five years. Flexible terms of office characterize many par-

DEGREES OF CONFIDENCE

In most of the majoritarian systems modeled on the British Parliament, the idea that a vote of non-confidence should be followed by the government's resignation is merely conventional, not a legally binding constitutional rule. In theory, governments could continue to try to govern following one or several such votes of non-confidence. In practice, though, if the legislature has truly lost confidence in the executive, continuing to govern will not be feasible, since it will not be possible for the government to gain approval for its legislation or its financial resolutions. In most other parliamentary systems, the requirement of resignation after defeat on a confidence vote has been constitutionalized. Here too, there are variations. In Finland, the President is not required to accept the resignation of the government, but may do so (and in practice, is unlikely not to do so). In France and Sweden, defeat of the government requires the vote of an absolute majority in the legislature (that is, a majority of all legislators, not just a majority of those present at the time of voting). In Germany, a motion of non-confidence in the Prime Minister must specify his or her successor. (Laver and Schofield, 1990)

FIGURE 2.6

liamentary systems and certainly all those that we have described as majoritarian.

To repeat, then, majority governments (almost always found in majoritarian systems) usually end at the time of their own choosing, either serving the maximum time constitutionally permitted, or choosing to face the electorate sooner because they believe they are currently well placed to win the election. The closer governments get to their constitutional deadline before calling an election the more likely it is that they are unpopular with the public and are simply delaying an inevitable defeat. Paradoxically, while serving the longest term is a measure of government stability or durability, it can in fact mask political weakness. The point to note is that if a majority government resigns there is little choice but to call an election, since no other party or combination of parties in the legislature can govern successfully.

The other (fairly) common reason for government changes in majority situations is because of a change in Prime Minister. This is typically a voluntary retirement, usually coming near the end of a term of office, but as demonstrated by the caucus revolt that replaced British Prime Minister Margaret Thatcher with John Major in 1990, or by the assassination of Swedish Prime Minister Olaf Palme in 1986, party revolt and death can remove incumbent prime ministers. In majoritarian systems with flexible terms, it is often expected that a Prime Minister sworn in without having faced the electorate as party leader will do so at the earliest possible opportunity, and so "earn" their mandate.

Minority governments can end for the same reasons as majority governments, but are much more likely to be finished by a defeat in the legislature, by a loss of confidence. With few exceptions, loss of a confidence motion means the end of the government in parliamentary regimes. One exception is Switzerland, where the executive, having passed the investiture vote, is not subject to legislative votes of confidence. A partial exception is Germany, where the legislature can terminate the government only with a vote of **CONSTRUCTIVE NON-CONFIDENCE**, which means that in addition to rejecting the current executive, the legislators must have agreed on a successor in whom they have confidence (see Figure 2.6). Not surprisingly, Budge and Keman's study of 20 democracies between 1950 and 1983 found that defeat in the legislature was the most frequent cause of termination for minority governments, and of all types of government, minority governments were most likely to be terminated by legislative defeat (see Figure 2.8).

TYPES OF EXECUTIVE COALITION

Various theories of coalition formation exist, some based on the premise that coalitions are driven by the desire of their members for power, some based on the premise that political parties seek particular policy outcomes first and foremost, and some combining both elements. In any case, these theories compare the strengths and weaknesses of different types of executive coalitions.

MINIMAL WINNING COALITION: This is a coalition that has as many parties as are necessary to control a majority of the legislature, no more. In the example below, any combination of parties that adds up to no less than 251 members and that cannot lose a member and still have no less than 251 members, is a minimal winning coalition: thus combinations AD, BD, ABC, and ABE are all minimal winning coalitions (there are other combinations, too), but BCD is not a minimal winning coalition because Party C's votes are not necessary to give control of a legislative majority.

MINIMUM WINNING COALITION: Depending on the number of parties and their relative strength there may be many minimal winning coalitions; the smallest of them is the minimum winning coalition. In our example this would be the government BD, with 265 legislators.

MINIMUM CONNECTED WINNING COALITION: We have ranged the parties ideologically below, and coalition theory expects a more stable government from partners closely aligned ideologically. Thus the minimum winning coalition BD joins two partners that are unconnected ideologically. In our example below there is only one minimal connected winning coalition: ABC, which is also therefore the minimum connected winning coalition.

SURPLUS MAJORITY COALITION: As we noted above, BCD is not a minimal winning coalition because Party C's votes could be lost without majority control of the legislature being compromised. Therefore Party C is an extra passenger. Surplus majority coalitions contain one or more surplus passengers. The government BD, which is a minimum winning coalition may be made more stable by adding party C, which makes the government partners ideologically connected.

GRAND COALITION: When a surplus majority coalition contains all significant parties in the legislature, it is called a grand coalition, and this usually exists for reasons of national unity, or in response to a state of national crisis. Governments ABCDE or ABCD would be grand coalitions in our example.

EXAMPLE

LEFT		CENTER		RIGHT
Party A	Party B	Party C	Party D	Party E
135	115	75	150	26

[Total seats: 501; Majority = 251]

FIGURE 2.7

Finally, in coalition government situations, a cause of government termination arises that is not so likely in single-party governments (majority or minority), namely internal cabinet dissension. As we have observed, cabinet government is a collective executive and the failure of cabinet members to work together and support a common policy platform signals an inability to govern. While this is possible but unlikely in single-party governments, given the mechanisms of party discipline, it is very possible once we have coalition (multi-party) governments. Although coalitions involve a formal agreement about portfolios and a policy platform, disagreements about either (let alone other factors such as personality clashes between party leaders) may arise during the life of a government. Failure to resolve these conflicts may lead to the collapse of the coalition, or its defeat in the legislature, and hence its resignation. The greater probability of internal collapse in coalition governments is the primary reason for their reputation for instability, especially as compared with single-party majority governments, and this is a key basis on which majoritarian and proportionate systems have been compared and evaluated. On this matter, a couple of observations are in order.

The stability of multi-party governments is itself highly variable, depending on several factors. One area of continuing interest and investigation is the kind of coalition formed, which has to do with the number of parties involved in government and their relationships to each other (ideology, relative strength) and to the rest of the legislature (size of majority, etc.). Some of the types of coalition are discussed in Figure 2.7, but otherwise this remains a topic beyond our scope here. Second, coalition stability depends greatly on the political culture, political practice, and institutional rules of individual nation-states. Two of the countries with the least stable coalitions—Fourth Republic France, and Italy from 1945 to 1996—also have had unique features that account in large part for their instability. One factor that has contributed to Italy's instability has been the fragmented party system and, prior to the 1990s, the attempt to exclude a large Communist Party from office at any cost. Also, the practice of secret legislative votes weakens the ability of party leaders to enforce discipline on their members. In countries like Switzerland and Germany, by contrast, coalition governments have been as stable as single-party majorities elsewhere. Collapse of a governing coalition is another cause of government termination that need not lead to an election; it may be quite feasible to put together a fresh partnership of parties from the legislature as it stands. In fact, in many cases, the collapse of a coalition has led to a new government identical to the previous in its party composition, but with a new PM, or key portfolios shuffled, or reconstituted on the basis of a newly negotiated policy platform. Behind the instability of coalition may stand a great deal of continuity.

The principal causes of government **TERMINATION** are shown in Figure 2.8, divided among the kinds of government, and the types of parliamentary system. We have, on the assumption that the resignation of the Prime Minister and constitutional intervention are causes of termination not related to the differences between type of system or type of government, collapsed these into the category "other," and indeed, there seems to be little difference

REASONS FOR TERMINATION OF PARLIAMENTARY GOVERNMENTS, 1950-1953

TYPE OF SYSTEM	ELECTION		POLITICAL		
	FIXED	ANTICIPATED	GOVERNMENT DISSENSION	LEGISLATIVE DISSENSION	OTHER
MAJORITARIAN (Australia, Britain, Canada, New Zealand)	44% (26)	24% (14)	5% (3)	8.5% (5)	18.5% (11) Total Cases = 59
PROPORTIONATE (Austria, Belgium, Denmark, Finland, France 4, France 5, Germany, Iceland, Ireland, Israel, Italy, Luxembourg, Netherlands, Norway, Sweden)	27% (81)	11% (32)	30% (90)	15% (44)	17% (51) Total Cases = 298
TYPE OF GOVERNMENT					
SINGLE-PARTY MAJORITY	48% (44)	19% (17)	9% (8)	5.5% (5)	19% (17) Total Cases = 91
COALITION	27% (46)	8% (13)	35% (60)	13.5% (23)	17% (29) Total Cases = 171
MINORITY	20% (19)	16% (15)	16% (15)	25% (23)	23% (21) Total Cases = 93
CARETAKER	32% (8)	24% (6)	36% (9)	4% (1)	4% (1) Total Cases = 25

Source: Adapted from Budge and Keman, 1990.

FIGURE 2.8

here between majoritarian and proportionate systems, or between majority, coalition, and minority governments. The key differences have rather to do with governments terminating for electoral reasons and governments terminating for what Keman and Budge call "political" reasons. In general the data show that governments in majoritarian systems are more likely to terminate because an election is required or is anticipated by the government, and less likely to terminate because of legislative defeat or internal cabinet conflict. Almost identical results are obtained for single-party majority governments, which is not surprising given that most of these will have occurred within majoritarian systems. Governments in proportionate systems are more likely to terminate for political reasons than for electoral reasons, and conflict between cabinet partners is the most frequent cause of termination; similar results show for coalition governments generally. Minority governments, by contrast, are more likely to be terminated by legislative defeat than are single-party majorities or coalitions.

2.3.4   THE HEAD OF STATE

In a parliamentary system, the head of state is a largely formal office, performing "a number of significant symbolic, procedural and diplomatic functions" (Gallagher et al., 1992: 14). In many cases the office of the head of state is a remnant of the traditional monarchy, or has evolved from modifications of the same. Of the 19 parliamentary democracies of Western Europe, the head of state in seven is a monarch, and in Luxembourg a grand duke; in the remainder the head of state is a president. Of the 11 Western European presidents, six are elected directly by the people, and five are elected by the people's representatives in the legislature. In four countries, the office of the head of state departs from the parliamentary norm in significant ways. In three countries (France, Finland, and Portugal, arranged in descending order of applicability) the President exercises discretionary power in ways more like the strong President within the U.S. separation of powers. In the remainder of the European parliamentary systems, heads of state perform largely ceremonial functions as described by Gallagher et al. We should perhaps note that in Canada, Australia, and New Zealand, the active head of state is a Governor-General who represents the sovereign — in each case the British monarch. In most of the newly minted democracies of Eastern Europe and the former Soviet Union, the head of state is a President: in many cases the "weak" or non-political President one normally associates with a parliamentary system, but in several regimes (e.g., Poland, Russia, the Ukraine, Belarus) the President has more formidable powers, thus combining parliamentary government with elements of strong presidentialism.

Beyond the symbolic and ceremonial roles of the head of state, this office serves two other political purposes. One has to do with the requirement that there always be a legal government in office; in most cases the most important political duty of the head of state is to see that this is so, whether this means an active role for the head of state in the government formation process, or implementing constitutionally prescribed procedures.[5] In either case the head of state is supposed to serve as the representative of the whole people, "above" partisan politics and serving no particular interest or interests. Where heads of state manage to maintain the public respect for their office by observing these conventions of political neutrality, they are also in a position to act or intervene in times of constitutional crisis or deadlock, and use their influence to ensure stability. A good example of this was the decisive role of King Juan Carlos in Spain's transition from a dictatorship to a liberal democracy in the mid-1970s. As with other dimensions of parliamentary politics, so, too, the role of the head of state may be somewhat different in majoritarian and proportionate systems.

In the normal course of things in a majoritarian system, the head of state will have little decision-making to do. If the electoral system returns a single-party majority to the legislature, then the leader of this party will be invited to form a government. Should the Prime Minister of a majority government present the government's resignation to the head of state and/or ask for a dissolution of the legislature and a new election, there is no basis for the head of state to refuse. In other words, if there is a single-party majority, the birth of the government is automatic, and its termination is in the control of the Prime Minister. In either case, the head of state merely fulfills necessary procedural requirements. When there is no party with a legislative majority, or such a majority evaporates, the situation of the head of state may be quite different — subject, of course, to the constitutional rules alluded to earlier.

2.3.5 THE POLITICAL EXECUTIVE: PRIME MINISTER AND CABINET

It should be clear by now that the central institution of the parliamentary system is the cabinet, and that the central figure in the cabinet is the Prime Minister. Under the leadership of the Prime Minister, the cabinet makes policy, presents it (where necessary) in the form of legislation to Parliament, and remains responsible for its implementation and administration by means of the agencies and departments of the state. The size, structure, and working styles of cabinet government vary from country to country, reflecting some of the differences in political culture, circumstances, and expectations that we have seen previously. At one extreme, the size and functioning is almost entirely at the discretion of the Prime Minister and will reflect his or her own style and philosophy of

5. One exception is Sweden, which has transferred this role to the speaker of the legislature.

PARLIAMENTARY HEADS OF STATE

A   MONARCHS
Belgium, Britain, Denmark, Luxembourg (Grand Duke), Netherlands, Norway, Spain, Sweden; exercised through a Governor-General: Australia, Canada, New Zealand.

B   (WEAK) PRESIDENTS
(a) directly elected: Austria, Iceland, Ireland
(b) elected by legislature: Germany, Greece, Italy, Malta, Switzerland

C   (STRONG) PRESIDENTS
(all directly elected): France, Finland, Portugal

FIGURE 2.9

governing. At the other pole, the size of cabinet is fixed in the constitution (e.g., in Switzerland it is set at seven members). Comparative study of cabinets and cabinet government has produced a large and growing body of literature in recent years.

The size of cabinets seems to depend greatly on two factors; the size of the state, and the size of the legislature. To take the latter first, the larger the legislature, the larger will be the group of supporters (whether from one party or several) on whom the government's life depends. It is obviously important to make sure a proper percentage of these supporters are rewarded for their loyalty with cabinet posts, or with parliamentary secretaryships, or other related positions of higher status (and usually higher pay, etc.). The smaller the cabinet (and related positions), the larger the body of potentially restless "backbenchers."[6] All other things being equal, we will expect that the larger the legislature (or the larger the winning party's caucus) the larger the cabinet will be. Figure 2.10 indicates that the largest postwar cabinets have been in the countries with the largest legislatures: Italy, France, and Britain. In fact, the British keep the cabinet smaller than it might otherwise be by distinguishing between the ministry, which includes all legislators sworn in as ministers of the Crown and thus exercising administrative responsibilities, and the cabinet, which is a special committee of senior ministers chaired by the PM.

The second factor having a large bearing on the size of cabinets has been the growth of the state, particularly in this century. An increase in the scope of government leads to new programs, new departments to implement and administer them, and thus to new ministries and portfolios. One could argue that this is not an inevitable development, that ministers could double up, taking responsibility for more than one portfolio, or that (as in Britain), not all department heads or administrators (i.e., ministers) need be considered in the cabinet. This is true, but it ignores the prestige that comes with cabinet status, and the importance of this means of reward to Prime Ministers seeking to consolidate their hold on a parliamentary caucus. All things being equal, then, as the size of the state increases, we would expect the size of cabinet also to grow.

Closely related to the size of cabinets is their structure. Generally speaking, the larger the cabinet, the more elaborate

SIZE OF PARLIAMENTARY CABINETS, 1945-90

COUNTRY	AVG. SIZE	RANGE OF SIZE
Italy	24	15 - 32
France (5th Rep.)	22	15 - 36
Britain	21	16 - 33
Belgium	20	15 - 27
France (4th Rep.)	19	13 - 26
Germany	18	13 - 22
Sweden	18	14 - 21
Denmark	17	12 - 22
Norway	16	13 - 19
Ireland	15	12 - 17
Netherlands	14	10 - 18
Austria	13	11 - 16
Finland	13	7 - 18
Luxembourg	8	6 - 10

Source: Steiner, 1995: 99.

FIGURE 2.10

6. So called because they sit on the back or rear benches in the House of Commons; cabinet ministers and their opposition critics sit on the front benches.

its structure will become. (It may well be that it is as much the other way around: the more structured the cabinet, the greater the incentive to appoint bodies to fill out the structure.) Obviously there is going to be a trade-off between cabinet size and the ease of decision-making: the larger the committee the more voices there are to be heard, the greater the potential difficulty of achieving consensus, etc.

The point this chronicle should emphasize is the pre-eminence of the Prime Minister. Not only are ministers appointed by the PM, and continue to serve at his or her pleasure, but it is the PM who may determine the size and structure of cabinet, decisions that will depend very much on his or her philosophy and leadership style. The complete dominance of the cabinet by the PM is something we would expect more of single-party governments, majority or minority, than of coalition cabinets, where questions of size, structure, and functioning will be part of the negotiated agreement among coalition partners. As Laver and Shepsle point out, cabinet decision-making is also very much a question of how "individual cabinet ministers are constrained by key political institutions" (1996: 5). Figure 2.11 presents various models of cabinet decision-making they discuss.

2.3.6 POLICY-MAKING: EXECUTIVE DOMINANCE

At this point a few remarks may be in order concerning the role of the cabinet and PM in policy-making. To put it baldly, in parliamentary systems the cabinet monopolizes policy-making. We have described responsible government as perhaps the distinguishing feature of parliamentary government, meaning specifically the requirement that the cabinet maintain the confidence of the legislature. Given the strength of party discipline in most countries, this confidence is virtually guaranteed for any party (or combination of parties) that controls a majority of the legislators in parliament. The result is that responsible government takes on a new meaning: namely that the cabinet is "responsible" for everything! Deciding what government will do, or not do, when it will be done and how; drafting regulations or legislation and presenting the latter to parliament; overseeing the implementation and ongoing administration of policy; all of these are in the control of the cabinet, and that leaves very little else. This is why parliamentary systems are usually described as having strong executive and weak legislatures,

MODELS OF CABINET DECISION-MAKING

EFFECTIVE POWER RESTS OUTSIDE THE EXECUTIVE

BUREAUCRATIC GOVERNMENT

The power to make public policy rests in this instance with the bureaucracy. In this case who is in cabinet or in control of the legislature makes little or no difference to policy.

LEGISLATIVE GOVERNMENT

The legislature makes policy and the cabinet's role is simply that of implementation.

EFFECTIVE POWER RESTS WITH THE EXECUTIVE

PRIME MINISTERIAL GOVERNMENT

Policy-making takes place within a collective executive dominated by the Prime Minister.

PARTY GOVERNMENT

The cabinet is subject to the parliamentary caucus, which can force policy options. Clearly this is most feasible in a single-party government.

CABINET GOVERNMENT

This is the classical counterpart of collective responsibility: a decision-making process that is also collective and is usually protected by conventions of confidentiality.

MINISTERIAL GOVERNMENT

In this model, one of autonomy within a collective executive, each minister has significant if not primary influence for policies that fall under his/her portfolio.

Source: Laver and Shepsle, 1996: 5-8.

FIGURE 2.11

or to put it another way, as being characterized by **EXECUTIVE DOMI-NANCE**. Executives may be more or less stable, depending on the status of its majority, or the nature of the coalition that comprises it, but whatever the composition of the government, the relative centrality of the cabinet within the system remains. This dominance is emphasized if we consider the principal challenges to it that exist.

Clearly the foundation upon which modern cabinet government rests is **CABINET SOLIDARITY** achieved through strong party discipline, and those parliaments with unstable coalitions are often those in which, for one reason or another, this coherence is lacking. This is the exception rather than the rule, because there is every incentive for parties to develop mechanisms to enforce discipline and thereby enhance the odds of their own political survival (an undisciplined party risks alienating an electorate uncertain of what it stands for). The sanctions that party leaders employ will be a mixture of inducements and punishments. The control that the cabinet and, more usually, the PM have over appointments (to judicial office, commissions, boards, even second chambers of the legislature) means an abundance of rewards for loyal behavior—quite apart from the hope of landing someday in cabinet, or even the PM's office. The penalties for disloyalty can be as varied, from exclusion from scarce positions of influence or additional remuneration, to exclusion from the party caucus (which, in those legislatures where the rules give privileges to parties, amounts to being silenced), to being dropped down or off the party's list of candidates for the next election. The effect of these mechanisms of party discipline is to internalize any dissent, and thus remove it from public view. This is one purpose of meetings of the party caucus (the parliamentary party); held behind closed doors, these meetings allow backbenchers to challenge the decisions of leaders, and in some cases have led to reversals on policy. More often than not, though, it appears that caucus functions to allow leaders to instruct backbenchers on what is expected of them: how they are to vote on issues, what the party's public position is on matters, etc. Successful internal challenge of cabinet dominance is rare in parliamentary systems.

A second possible challenge to the dominance of the cabinet is the presence of a strong second chamber in those systems with bicameral (literally, "two house") legislatures, especially when the powers of the two houses are equal or symmetrical. As we have seen, responsible government directs the attention of the cabinet to the popularly elected or "first" chamber of the legislature. It is also with respect to the behavior of members in this chamber that party discipline will be most effective. In bicameral legislatures it is possible that the party (or coalition) that controls the first chamber (and the cabinet) does not have a majority in the second chamber, or is less able to control party members in this chamber. Where this is so, the constitutional powers of the second chamber will make a clear difference to the dominance of the cabinet. If the second chamber has weak powers, the cabinet will not be seriously challenged by its dissent; if its powers are strong, the cabinet may well find here an effective opposition. Where the second chamber has the ability to veto or block legislation coming from the first chamber it will be in a position of potential challenger to the government. As Lijphart notes, this is enhanced by having the second chamber represent a different constituency, or be (s)elected on a different basis from the first chamber. Of the world's democracies, he judges four to satisfy these twin conditions of **STRONG** or **SYMMETRICAL BICAMERALISM** : Australia, Germany, Switzerland, and (as we have seen) the United States. The latter, of course, is not parliamentary and, as we have noted, Switzerland represents a rather exceptional case in several respects. In short, in most parliamentary democracies, the second chamber does not present an effective opposition to cabinet government.

A third possibility is the addition of a strong presidency to what is otherwise a system of responsible parliamentary government. This has been the experience in Western Europe of France (Fifth Republic) and to a lesser extent Finland; and in Eastern Europe of several fledgling democracies, most notably Poland and Russia. These are exceptions to the parliamentary norm, and we will explore in the next chapter the reasons for creating a strong head of state in parliamentary systems. In most cases, however, this has not been to oppose an over-strong cabinet government, but to provide stability to weak multi-party systems.

In normal circumstances, then, parliamentary government means a relatively unhampered executive dominance over the legislature, and a relatively coherent control by the cabinet of policy-making and implementation. This means that parliamentary government is, all else being equal, *strong* government, able—if it is willing—to put the power of the state behind the problem-solving it undertakes (not that this guarantees a solution). The ability of parliamentary government to act decisively and quickly is one of its advantages among democratic systems. This does *not* mean that parliamentary government is absolute; there are at least two other possible checks on the policy-making of cabinet government. One (although absent in many parliamentary constitutions) is the judicial review of legislation, or other constitutional judgments issued by the high courts concerning government actions. Where judicial review is possible, merely the possibility of its taking place may constrain governments from certain policies. Ultimately, though, the judgment that no cabinet government in a parliamentary democracy can escape is that of the people. Periodic, competitive elections offer citizens the opportunity to register their approval and disapproval of government policies and to replace one government with another. One could argue, in fact, that only on the premise that the political process delivers effective popular control over government can the powerful centralization of power in the hands of cabinet government be justified. Where this premise is false, there is little that parliamentary government cannot do and, as in earlier days, citizens must rely on the wisdom and moral restraint of their rulers.

As we have noted, in normal parliamentary constitutions, the role of the head of state is largely formal: that is, ceremonial and procedural. It is the Prime Minister who exercises political authority as head of government (i.e., chair of cabinet). It is not difficult to imagine (although we will explain it more precisely in a moment) a situation where the head of state retains, or is allocated, some of the political authority or discretionary powers that would otherwise fall to the Prime Minister. The question is: why do it?

In the case of France's Fifth Republic (in place since 1958), the universal answer is that the creation of a strong presidency was an answer to the instability of the Fourth Republic (1946-58). In the 13 years of the Fourth Republic, France had 27 governments, beset with an overly fragmented party system and unstable coalitions further destabilized by divisive foreign policy questions, in particular the issue of Algerian independence. The constitution of the Fifth Republic, authored by Charles DeGaulle (its first President) and Michel Debré (the future Prime Minister), weakened the role of parliament and Prime Minister, and strengthened the presidency in several important ways, thus creating a unique dual executive or **DYARCHY**.

Since 1962, the President has been elected directly by the French people, initially to a seven-year term, a lengthy period in office intended to ensure that the executive would be a stable institution independent of possible parliamentary turnover or turmoil. In September 2001 President Jacques Chirac called a referendum to change the constitution so as to shorten the term to five years. The shorter term makes it less likely that a President winning majority support would face a parliament of a different partisan stripe. The President, in turn, appoints the Prime Minister and, depending on circumstances, the cabinet ministers. If sitting members of the legislature are appointed to cabinet, they must resign their legislative seats. The government, once installed, is responsible to the first chamber of the legislature, the National Assembly. A motion of censure (non-confidence) must be moved by at least one-tenth of the Assembly's deputies, and to succeed requires the approval of an absolute majority. The President also has the ability to dissolve parliament at any time and require elections, and may also dismiss the Prime Minister at will. In these,

2.4
Presidentialism in Parliamentary Systems: France as a Hybrid

and several other ways, the French President has considerable control over both the government and the legislature. In addition, although the practice has fallen into disuse, the President has the ability to circumvent parliament and put questions directly to the people in a referendum. The French chief executive also has considerable emergency powers, and, like the American President, is commander-in-chief of the armed forces. Certainly, the office of President is much stronger in France than the United States given the control the French President wields over the legislature. On the other hand, the French President enjoys an independence from the legislature and a direct mandate conferred through popular election that parliamentary prime ministers lack.

Having said this, we should note that the pre-eminence of the French President is at its zenith when his political party also controls a majority in the legislature, a circumstance that has been the norm for most of the Fifth Republic. Some observers even doubted if this system of a dual executive could work if there were to be a strong parliamentary majority opposed to the President. However, successful **COHABITATION** between a socialist President and a conservative Prime Minister and government occurred on two separate occasions during the 14 years of Mitterand's two-term presidency. While the President appoints the Prime Minister, the realities of parliament do constrain this choice, especially when the electorate has given a clear mandate to one party or group of like-minded parties. One of Mitterand's greatest accomplishments may have been his demonstration, through his handling of conservative Prime Ministers Jacques Chirac and later Edouard Balladur, that the Fifth Republic system of a dual executive can work in France. In part, this has been true because of a willingness to recognize that the balance of power within the executive can shift between Prime Minister and President as circumstances vary. In fact, the party roles were reversed when cohabitation occurred again between the conservative President Jacques Chirac and socialist Prime Minister Lionel Jospin from 1997 to 2002.

In France, as elsewhere, there is a difference between the formal or legal constitution and what we have called the constitution as the actual structure of authority—what Sartori calls the *material constitution*. It is worth noting that in the French constitution, the primary responsibility for public policy rests with the Prime Minister and cabinet. In practice, though, especially under de Gaulle, the material constitution was one in which the President's will prevailed over the Prime Minister and government. In describing "semi-presidential" systems, of which he believes France is the exemplar, Sartori makes the useful observation that the president "is not entitled to govern alone or directly, and therefore his will must be conveyed and processed via his government" (1994: 132). In this way it is possible to understand how, when the government comes from the President's party, the preponderance of policy-making power may rest with the President rather than the Prime Minister. Conversely, when the government comes from a party ideologically opposed to the President (as the government must when such a party clearly controls the legislature), the ability of the President to express his will via the government will be constrained. In these circumstances the Prime Minister's influence over policy-making is enhanced, or so Mitterand seemed to understand during his two periods of cohabitation with an ideological rival in government. When there is a double majority (the same party controls the presidency and the legislature), the material constitution tends to be in effect, and the President dominates. With both President and parliament on the same five-year electoral schedule, periods of cohabitation are much less likely since both branches are likely to be elected at the same time. If a President is elected and lacks parliamentary support, she or he can simply dissolve the National Assembly and call parliamentary elections. This is, of course, exactly what current President Jacques Chirac did following his May 2002 victory and the French electorate complied by returning a majority for the mainstream right parties supportive of Chirac in June 2002. When there is a split majority, the formal constitution, which assigns policy to the Prime Minister and government, is adhered to more closely.

There is good reason to see the French union of a strong presidency with a parliamentary system as something idiosyncratic, designed to meet the particular problems and requirements of France, and managing to work within the political traditions and culture of France. Finland is often described as another parliamentary system with strong presidentialism. As in France, the Finnish president appoints the Prime Minister and can dissolve parliament and require elections. As in other countries, the Finnish President has particular responsibility for the country's foreign relations and chairs cabinet meetings dealing with such issues. In other policy areas, Finland functions as a normal parliamentary system. One ambiguity in the Finnish case is the election of the President: since 1988 direct election occurs if a candidate achieves a majority of the vote; if no candidate achieves this majority, an indirect procedure is resorted to, which has the effect of undermining the legitimacy of the office. Whatever its constitutional status, the Finnish chief executive has been much less powerful in practice than his/her French counterpart.

As we have indicated earlier, strong presidents also exist in parliamentary systems in several of the new democracies to emerge from Eastern Europe and the former Soviet Union. As these are all less than two decades old, it is premature to pass judgment on their effectiveness, and in many cases the exact nature of the relationship between presidency and the parliamentary executive is still not clear, or is clearly still evolving. The rationale for having a strong presidency in these countries is once again to counteract potential or perceived instability in the political system. In most of these countries, authoritarian regimes were in place for a considerable period, which means that the political culture has not developed or sustained the attitudes and practices that are associated with democratic politics. Similarly, political pluralism is also new to these regimes; once officially one-party systems, free elections have now produced extremely fragmented multi-party systems. In Poland, for example, the first truly free parliamentary elections returned 29 parties to the Sejm (Poland's legislature), the largest winning only 13.5 per cent of the seats. Over time, in such regimes, one expects parties with similar ideological leanings to merge and consolidate their support, while other parties (such as Poland's Beer Lovers Party) may eventually disappear. Clearly though, forming a government in such fragmented parliaments is a challenge, and sustaining a coalition is always more difficult the more fragmented the party system. Not surprisingly, Polish President Lech Walesa and Russia's Boris Yeltsin (and more recently, Vladimir Putin) tried to emulate the French presidency in the early stages of their newly emerging democracies. Whether a strong presidency is merely a temporary expedient for these parliamentary systems until they establish institutional stability and loyalty to democratic traditions, or something that will persist as in the French Fifth Republic to date, is something too early to judge.

**2.5
Conclusion**

The weakness of a presidential system with separated powers was one of its attractions for those who designed it, insofar as they wished to avoid absolutism and tyranny. Such systems are likely to be preferred by anyone who wishes to minimize the role for government and maximize the scope for private (individual) freedom. It also means that policy-making can be difficult and is often stymied by stalemate. As we noted earlier, the successful export of the American system to other countries has been rare. Sartori (1994) lists 18 countries outside the U.S. with presidential democracies; apart from the Philippines, all are in Latin America, and only three—Costa Rica (1949), Venezuela (1958), and Colombia (1974)—have been uninterruptedly democratic for more than 20 years (and even here, Venezuela experienced a short-lived coup d'état in early 2002, and Colombia is struggling to maintain internal order against a variety of guerrilla forces). Sartori (1994: 89) concludes:

> Ironically, then, the belief that presidential systems are strong systems draws on the worst possible structural arrangements—a divided power defenseless against divided government—and fails to realize that the American system works, or has worked, *in spite* of its constitution—hardly *thanks to* its constitution.

One reason for mistaking the presidential system as strong may be the misperceptions of the *American* president (i.e., as world leader, military commander, etc.) alluded to above. Another may be the misidentification of those systems where a strong president adds stability to (or is intended to stabilize) a parliamentary regime.

What we have glimpsed in this chapter is the great variety of constitutional arrangements that can structure relationships between executives and legislatures within systems that otherwise have a great deal in common. Common to presidential systems is the feature that political executives are not drawn from and/or are not responsible to legislatures. It remains the case that apart from the U.S. and the few stable Latin American examples of U.S.-style separation-of-powers systems, the world's democratic nations have followed the parliamentary route. In a distinct minority of cases, this has been a presidentialism without a separation of powers, and for that reason this weak form of presidentialism that might evolve into something resembling the more passive head of state we typically associate with "normal" parliamentary regimes. Portugal, for example, has abandoned its flirtation with strong presidentialism, and it may be that other systems with strong presidents might do so, also, as they stabilize. At the end of the day we are left with a great variety of parliamentary systems, so much so that for almost every generalization we can offer, there is at least one exception to the rule. The strongest distinction remains that between systems that put power in the hands of one party (majoritarian), and those that tend to produce coalitions (proportionate). In the next chapter we will turn to a wholly different basis for distinguishing among democratic polities, namely the extent to which political powers are concentrated in the national governments or decentralized through subnational levels of government.

REFERENCES AND SUGGESTED READING

Budge, Ian, and Hans Keman. 1990. *Parties and Democracy: Coalition Formation and Government Functioning in Twenty States.* Oxford: Oxford University Press.

Gallagher, Michael, et al. 1995. *Representative Government in Modern Europe*, 2nd ed. New York: McGraw-Hill.

Lane, Jan-Erik, and Svante O. Errson. 1991. *Politics and Society in Western Europe*, 2nd ed. Newbury Park, CA: Sage.

Laver, Michael, and Norman Schofield. 1990. *Multiparty Government: The Politics of Coalition in Europe.* Oxford: Oxford University Press.

——. and Kenneth A. Shepsle. 1996. *Making and Breaking Governments.* Cambridge: Cambridge University Press.

Lijphart, Arend. 1984. *Democracies: Patterns of Majoritarian and Consensus Government in Twenty-One Countries.* New Haven: Yale University Press.

——, ed. 1992. *Parliamentary versus Presidential Government.* Oxford: Oxford University Press.

Mahler, Gregory. 1992. *Comparative Politics: An Institutional and Cross-National Perspective.* Englewood Cliffs, NJ: Prentice-Hall.

Mény, Yves. 1993. *Government and Politics in Western Europe.* Oxford: Oxford University Press.

Müller, Wolfgang C., and Kaare Strøm, eds. 2000. *Coalition Governments in Western Europe.* Oxford: Oxford University Press.

Neustadt, Richard. 1986. *Presidential Power.* New York: Wiley.

Parenti, Michael. 1978. *Power and the Powerless.* New York: St. Martin's Press.

——. 1980. *Democracy for the Few*, 3rd ed. New York: St. Martin's Press.

Redman, Eric. 1973. *The Dance of Legislation.* New York: Simon & Shuster.

Riggs, Fred W. 1994. "Conceptual Homogenization in a Heterogeneous Field: Presidentialism in Comparative Perspective," in Mattei Dogan and Ali Kazancigil, eds., *Comparing Nations: Concepts, Strategies, Substance.* Oxford: Blackwell, 72-152.

Rossiter, Clinton, ed. 1961. *The Federalist Papers.* New York: Mentor.

Sartori, Giovanni. 1994. *Comparative Constitutional Engineering.* New York: New York University Press.

Steiner, Jurg. 1995. *European Democracies*, 3rd ed. New York: Longmans.

Zeigler, Harmon. 1990. *The Political Community.* New York: Longmans.

KEY TERMS

the "Administration"
cabinet solidarity
caretaker government
coalition government
cohabitation
constructive non-confidence
dissolution
dyarchy
electoral coalition
electoral parties
electoral system
executive coalition
executive dominance
formateur
government formation
grand coalition
inner cabinet
legislative coalition
legislative parties
majoritarian system
majority government
manufactured majority
minority government
parliamentary party
party system
pluralist democracy
plurality system
pocket veto
portfolio
presidentialism
proportionate representation system
strong or symmetrical bicameralism
termination
veto

THREE | Governing Territory: Unitary and Federal Systems

A federation is the most geographically expressive of all political systems. It is based on the existence of regional difference, and recognizes the claims of the component areas to perpetuate their individual characters...

Federation does not create unity out of diversity; rather, it enables the two to coexist.

— Kenneth Robinson

Thus far we have tended to speak about *the* state, or *the* government. However, in many countries people elect representatives to at least three and often more "nested" levels of government (local and/or county, state or province, and national or federal governments). Clearly governments are numerous. A recent census of U.S. governments shows that in addition to the federal government and those of the 50 states, there are 87,849 governments in the United States (U.S. Census Bureau, July 2002). The division of responsibilities and jurisdictions across these various levels of government constitutes an important feature of our political life that must be understood. As we shall see, America is not exceptional in this regard. This chapter deals with the feature that in almost every country the state exists at different levels, and rarely are people subject to only one government. Countries vary, however, according to the amounts of power they distribute to each of these levels of government, and in the institutional and legal mechanisms by which they distribute it. Some countries centralize most power in the hands of national (i.e., country-wide) political actors and processes. Others **DECENTRALIZE** large amounts of power to subnational units of government. This territorial distribution of power is independent of the type of democratic system (parliamentary

3.1 Introduction: Decentralization and Centralization

3.1 Introduction: Decentralization and Centralization

3.2 Definitions: Federal, Confederal, and Unitary Systems

3.3 Why Federalism?

3.4 The Division of Powers

   3.4.1 Legislative Powers

   3.4.2 Administrative Powers

   3.4.3 Fiscal Powers

3.5 Bicameralism in Federal States

3.6 Home Rule and Decentralization in Unitary States

3.7 Supranational Federalism: The European Union

or presidential) that we have been discussing, and merits a separate treatment.

We will review a number of options that countries face concerning the territorial distribution of power. Extreme centralization and extreme decentralization represent only the end-points on a continuum representing the territorial concentration or fragmentation of political power. A virtually infinite array of choices between these extremes is available to states. Choices with respect to the territorial distribution of power reflect a balancing of several important considerations. First, since almost all countries are large enough to contain significant geographic variations, there is a natural desire to provide citizens with outlets beneath the country-wide institutions of government through which they can attend to their particular needs and desires. By the same token, however, too much decentralization may threaten the very survival of the country by encouraging citizens to identify first and foremost as members of their local or subnational community rather than with the country as a whole. All states must strike a balance between centripetal and centrifugal tendencies and thereby achieve something approaching an optimal territorial distribution of powers given what is shared and what is geographically differentiated among their citizens. This is a complex and dynamic undertaking, for what is acceptable or optimal at one period in time may not remain so for long.

3.2
Definitions:
Federal, Confederal,
and Unitary Systems

A number of institutional arrangements that consolidate particular patterns of centralization and decentralization have been adopted by groups of states in the world today. This section establishes the core definitions of three general forms of territorial governance; confederal, federal, and unitary systems. In this respect, it is important to distinguish between a constitutional division of sovereignty across various levels of government and a simple decision on the part of one level voluntarily to share power with (or delegate authority to) other levels of government. Whereas the former divisions are more difficult to change, the latter can be modified arbitrarily by the level that retains sovereignty. The three terms defined in this section represent the primary choices in the constitutional division of powers. In general, the forms of government they represent can be ordered from the most decentralized types of loosely integrated and largely autonomous states (confederal systems) to the highly centralized states that leave most power to be exercised by country-wide political institutions that produce decisions for all citizens.

Where there is only one sovereign level of government, that is, where all subordinate levels exercise delegated authority, a **UNITARY STATE** exists, as in Great Britain, where all sovereignty ultimately rests with Parliament. At the other extreme is a situation where the regional or subnational governments are supreme, and the national authority is entirely their creation and servant. Such is a **CONFEDERATION**, and although the first Constitution of the United States embodied confederal principles, none exist in the world today. Between these two poles, a unitary state at one end, and a confederal state at the other, are all federal states, where each of the two levels of government is sovereign in some respect(s). Within this condition, there is an enormous range of possibilities, from systems where the weight of the central government is so dominant that it might as well be unitary (hence very *central- ized*), to such a weak central government that it might as well be confederal (hence very *decentralized*). Thus we might present the possibilities as follows:

UNITARY	FEDERAL			CONFEDERAL
CENTRAL	▲			central
▼	CENTRAL/ regional	CENTRAL/ REGIONAL	central/ REGIONAL	▲
local/regional				REGIONAL

On the other hand, what this obscures is the real possibility within what are constitutionally unitary states for a considerable decentralization of authority through delegation to regional and/or municipal governments. In this way a formally unitary constitution might in fact allow a division of power much more decentralized than a federal constitution where the central government has clear dominance. The distinction we made earlier between material and formal constitutions is useful here, too. While the authority of subordinate governments may in fact be delegated, and this means it may be revoked legally or altered by the central government, the limitations imposed by the political traditions, expectations, fiscal realities, etc. may impose limits on the practical ability of the central government to re-occupy areas of jurisdiction once delegated.

Federalism seems to be one of the political terms most difficult to define—see Figure 3.1—and yet what most definitions seem to share comes down to three elements:

1. the state is divided between a national government and regional or subnational governments,

2. the powers of government are constitutionally allocated between these two levels of government, and

3. each level of government possesses some autonomy from the other, meaning that neither can destroy the other, that each has the final say in some area(s) of jurisdiction, or both.

DEFINITIONS OF FEDERALISM

Federalism is a political organization in which the activities of government are divided between regional government and a central government in such a way that each kind of government has some activities on which it makes final decisions.
— William H. Riker, in Greenstein and Polsby, 1975: 101

A federal system of government consists of autonomous units that are tied together within one country.
— Steiner, 1995: 123

In a formal sense, federalism can be defined as a division of powers between central and regional governments such that neither is subordinate to the other.
— Dyck, 1996: 69

In a federal system there are two levels of government above the local level, each enjoying sovereignty in certain specific areas.
— Mahler, 1995: 31

It is a political system in which most or all of the structural elements of the state ... are duplicated at two levels, with both sets of structures exercising effective control over the same territory and population. Furthermore, neither set of structures should be able to abolish the other's jurisdiction over this territory or population.
— Stevenson, 1989: 8

[Federalism is] the method of dividing powers so that the general and regional governments are each, within a sphere, co-ordinate and independent.
— Wheare, 1963: 11

FIGURE 3.1

As noted, authority exists at more than one level in virtually every country (excepting perhaps micro-states or city-states); what makes for federalism—in our view—is the constitutional independence of two levels of government. The government of the United States cannot abolish the states, nor can the states dissolve the federal government. Municipal or local governments, by contrast, are entirely creatures of state governments. The authority to make or abolish municipal governments is one of the powers of the state level of government in the American Constitution. One way to understand this distinction is the notion of **DELEGATION**. Authority is delegated when it is transferred from one body to another, but the original body retains the right to take the authority back at any point in the future. Most of the authority that is exercised by public servants working in government bureaucracies is power delegated by the legislature, which in theory, could revoke it at any time. Delegated authority or power is on loan, however permanent this may seem. Municipal government is typically, as in the United States, delegated from a higher level of government. Federalism, by contrast, means two levels of government, each of which exercises authority not delegated by the other.

It is also noteworthy that the federal dimension of a constitution is one that can be subject to considerable evolution or development over time. The United States began as a confederation, re-constitutionalized as a relatively decentralized federation, and became by the mid-twentieth century much more

76

centralized than the Founding Fathers would ever have dreamed possible (or wise). By contrast, Canada began as a very centralized system, so much so that it was characterized by observers as (and formally, still is) **QUASI-FEDERAL**; in practice, it is now one of the world's most decentralized federations. Why federal systems are so flexible is something we will discuss after looking at the component features of federal constitutions. After discussing the features of systems that satisfy the definition of federalism, we will look at quasi-federal elements (including home rule), and then at decentralization within unitary states. What we must do first, though, is establish the rationale for structuring the state at more than one level.

W riting in 1995, Gregory Mahler noted that of 178 nation-states in the world, only 21 claimed to be federal, but included in these were five of the world's six largest countries (Russia, Canada, the United States, Brazil, and Australia); he also noted that China, which is not federal, nonetheless has some federal characteristics (1995: 31). Intuitively, it makes sense that *larger countries* would have more than one level of government; to govern from one center is simply not efficient or prudent. While administrative decentralization can achieve efficiency without creating an autonomous second level of government, in many cases the latter was often preferable, especially in the days before modern communication and transportation. Territorially based *cultural or linguistic minorities* often provided a rationale for decentralization and/or federalism, as these groups often demanded autonomy from centralizing and homogenizing policies. This was the case in Canada, where English and French communities had to be brought together in the process of state-formation. Switzerland, with its four linguistic communities, is an even more striking example than Canada of a country that has employed federalism to safeguard cultural entities. Political and social tensions based on linguistic and cultural difference have also transformed Belgium from a unitary state to an extremely decentralized federal state. *Historical factors* also contribute to the rationale for federalism. A very simple reason that large countries are likely to be federal is that they often are the product of a union of smaller territories, colonies, or even countries that have wished to retain some measure of autonomy in the new polity, and have achieved this through regional or subnational governments. Two other powerful incentives for such separate entities to unite are *economic reasons* (to create a viable or competitive market or to secure access to necessary resources), and fear of a *common foreign enemy* (or potential enemy).

3.3
Why Federalism?

UNITS OF FEDERALISM

The national level of government in federal systems is sometimes called the central government, or the national government, or, as in Canada, the federal government. The subnational or regional governments go by a variety of names:

Canada	Provinces
Germany	Länder
Switzerland	Cantons
United States	States
Brazil	States
India	States
Australia	States

FIGURE 3.2

It should be obvious by this point that federalism, if it entails the autonomy of both levels of government, will require a written constitution where this autonomy is articulated and entrenched. One of the devices we will expect in a federal constitution is a division of powers between the two levels of government. Among the powers so divided will be the ability to make laws in certain fields (i.e., jurisdictions), the power of administering laws, and the capacity to raise and spend money. This division is what is sometimes called the "federal bargain" between the two levels of government, and in a truly federal system, neither level of government can alter the federal bargain without the consent of the other level.

3.4.1 LEGISLATIVE POWERS

Let us begin with the division of legislative powers, the core of any federal constitution. Here a comparison of the American and Canadian experiences is particularly instructive, since despite the obvious similarities between these countries, the two federal systems formed under quite different circumstances and followed different developmental paths over time. The term "division of powers" suggests that there is a fixed set of jurisdictions we can simply apportion in some way (like a deck of cards, or Grandma's china) between two parties. In fact it turns out that dividing powers between levels of government is more difficult than this, and it is problematic with respect both to the principle(s) on which the division is based, and to the means used to accomplish it. Consider the principle first; one might assume it is simply a matter of assigning matters with a national dimension to the central government, and matters of a regional nature to the subnational governments. But what constitutes a "national" matter (and remember we are dealing with *subjects* of legislation, not particular cases)? Some matters, such as defense, foreign trade, treaties with foreign powers, minting currency, the postal service, etc., seem obviously national in character, and we would be surprised at finding them not assigned to the central government. Other subjects are not so clearcut: the regulation of labor relations, the environment, building and maintaining highways, education—in each of these cases an argument could be made either way, and in the real world these are sometimes national and sometimes regional responsibilities.

Matters are also complicated by the fact that the division of powers is a prime means of establishing which level of government will predominate—that is, how centralized or decentralized the system will be. When constitution framers want a centralized constitution, as the "Fathers of Confederation" did in Canada, they will try to give as many of the powers, or certainly what they believe to be the most important powers, to the national government. By contrast, in Switzerland, which was originally (and is nominally still) a confederation, the cantons are in theory "sovereign" and legislate in most areas according to their internal constitutions. It often turns out that whether you see something as a national or provincial matter depends on which level of government you happen to favor! As we have already noted, federal systems also have a remarkable capacity to evolve (within a constitutional division of powers) from decentralized to centralized systems, and vice versa.

Assuming that one can establish a principle of dividing the powers between the two levels of government, the means of indicating this in the constitution are various. Put most simply, the headings of power (the subjects concerning which a government may make law: that is, jurisdictions) must be enumerated in the constitution for one, or the other, or both levels of government. The simplest approach is to enumerate the powers of one level of government, and indicate that everything else belongs to its counterpart. By and large this is the approach of the American Constitution, which enumerates the powers of the national government, places certain prohibitions on the national, and state governments, respectively, and indicates that all other powers "are reserved to the States, respectively, or to the people" (Tenth Amendment). The Tenth Amendment is an example of a **RESIDUAL CLAUSE** (or "reservation clause"), which indicates the level of government that will receive powers not expressly allocated in the constitution. This is an important device, since constitution-makers will not list every possible area of government activity, especially those yet to be invented! For example, the American Constitution pre-dates the invention of air travel, telecommunications, and nuclear power, each of which require regulation by the state at some level. In the American case, then, the powers of the states are not enumerated, but residual, which on some interpretations at least, implies state supremacy. On the other hand, in addition to its enumerated powers the government of the United States is given the power "to make all laws which shall be necessary and proper" for carrying out its enumerated powers (the so-called "elastic clause" of Section 8, Article I), something open possibly to a very wide interpretation. In Canada, the federal constitution adopted in 1867 gave the federal government the right to legislate for "the Peace, Order, and Good Government" of the country.

In Germany, the regional governments, the *Länder*, hold the residual power under Article 70 of the Basic Law, which means the power to legislate in areas not expressly granted to the federal government. In addition, and an element with no Canadian or American parallel, the *Länder* can also legislate in the expressly federal areas when and to the degree that the federal government has declined to do so (Article 72). On the other hand, three separate reasons that justify the federal government's taking over a legislative field from the *Länder*, mean that the jurisdictions of the latter, while exclusive, are hardly secure (see Mény, 1993: 201). The net result is a very large area of concurrent jurisdiction, over which ultimately the federal government has final say. As we will see below, the balance between the German federal state and the *Länder* is more a function of the bicameral legislature than of the division of legislative powers.

The German example illustrates the possibility of **CONCURRENT** legislation, where both levels of government may occupy a field of jurisdiction. In the United States, Article 6, clause 2 (the "supremacy clause"), which states that "This Constitution, and the Laws of the United States ... shall be the supreme Law of the Land," is regarded as implying federal paramountcy. Section 109 of the Australian constitution explicitly states federal paramountcy, and the courts have adopted the same principle in Canada. If provincial and federal laws should conflict, the constitution specifies that the federal law will prevail. **PARAMOUNTCY** is not restricted to cases of concurrent jurisdiction. It might be that the levels of government, each legislating within its constitutionally defined **JURISDICTIONS**, come into conflict. In this instance, which law will prevail?

One point that deserves some attention is the tendency of federal constitutions to deviate from their original form, or from the balance originally intended. Canada, originally conceived as a very centralized federation, has become one of the world's most decentralized federal systems, while it is generally agreed that the United States has evolved in the opposite direction: from decentralized to centralized (or at least potentially so). In the course of this evolution, Americans put down a secessionist attempt from southern states in 1865. Canada has at times confronted a serious political problem stemming from the nationalist aspirations of a significant proportion of French-speakers living in the province of Quebec. Having risen sharply since the 1960s, the tide of support for an independent state of Quebec appears to have subsided somewhat since the 1995 referendum on independence. At that time, the prospect of independence was rejected by the narrowest of margins (50.4 per cent to 49.5 per cent; a difference of only several thousand votes). Despite the recent downturn in support, separatist forces are unlikely to disappear and movement leaders promise to hold more referenda until they are successful in obtaining independence for the province. How could these neighbors evolve so differently in their pattern of territorial governance?

There are several factors at work here. Obviously the character of a federal bargain can be altered deliberately through constitutional **AMENDMENT**, although this is made less likely by the requirement that such an amendment obtain the consent of both levels of government. In the United States, the Fourteenth, Sixteenth, and Seventeenth Amendments to the Constitution are seen to have limited states' rights.

By declaring a subject to be within (*intra vires*) or beyond (*ultra vires*) the **JURISDICTION** of one or the other level of government, Supreme Courts can transform the federal bargain, or indeed, halt its evolution. During the Depression of the 1930s in both Canada and the U.S., the Supreme Court ruled unconstitutional extensive social and economic legislation of the federal government on grounds that it encroached on the powers of the provinces and states, respectively. In fact, in both countries, there have been extended periods in which rulings from the Court have tended to favor the expansion of the relative power of one level of government or the other. It should also be noted that these cases often were the result of individuals challenging the jurisdictional constitutionality of a law, and not because one level of government was objecting to actions by the other.

Another important factor in the evolution of federalism has been socio-economic change. As a result of new technologies or a changing economic structure or demographic transformation, powers that once seemed central or important to constitution-framers become less important and matters once regarded as minor (or not yet foreseen) become of great importance. In Canada, for example, many areas were originally assigned to the provinces in the belief they were not areas of national importance nor requiring much government expenditure. Because of technological and social change, two such policy fields, health care and education, have become among the largest areas of government program spending. Similarly, roads and highways, which have ended up under provincial jurisdiction, had a much different significance in the days before the invention of the automobile.

Finally, we should note that the relative weights of the levels of state within a federation will depend to a considerable degree also on the use that governments make of the powers the constitution gives them, or of opportunities to expand or extend the boundaries of these powers. In the U.S., Roosevelt continued to push for expanded governmental powers despite rejection by the Supreme Court of his New Deal legislation, and after 1937 met with success. In Canada, decentralization occurred in part at least because strong provincial leaders were unwilling to have their governments play the merely local role that centralists such as Canada's first prime minister, John A. Macdonald, had envisaged in 1867. As we have noted, the extent of the power of the German *Länder* is very much a function of the decision by the federal government to act in a field. Much of the twentieth century witnessed the tremendous expansion of government, and in most federal countries, this occurred at both levels of the state: national and subnational. The last decade or so has been marked by a retreat of government in the face of massive accumulated debts. In most cases this has meant a downsizing of government activity and spending (or at least a reduction in the rate of growth), but not necessarily a change in *constitutional* powers. Nonetheless, in some cases, levels of government may look to offload responsibilities to their counterpart. This may be particularly relevant in cases, as we will see below, where the government's capacity to raise revenue does not match its spending responsibilities.

In short, a variety of factors combine to shape the ongoing evolution of the federal bargain within federal systems. The fact that this may lead to a deviation from the original settlement of powers upon the governments by the constitution does not make it wrong, or right. It just happens, and what matters more than its fidelity to the intentions of "founding fathers" is its effect on the ability of the two levels of government to be responsive to the problems of their common citizenry.

3.4.2 ADMINISTRATIVE POWERS

The American and Canadian constitutions appear to assume that it is normal for the level of government that makes laws in a particular field also to administer legislation in that jurisdiction. Such is not the case in Germany, where Article 84 of the Basic Law establishes that the *Länder* will implement and administer laws passed by the federal government. Not only is the executive responsibility for most (if not all) law passed to the *Länder*, but according to Article 83 of the Basic Law the *Länder* are empowered to execute federal laws "as matters of their own concern" (Mény, 1993: 209). This allows for considerable policy variance among the *Länder*, for how a program is delivered is very often as significant as any variable in determining its success. In this way, then, the legislative dominance of the German federal government is balanced by the administrative monopoly of the *Länder*. In 1998, *Länder* public servants outnumbered federal public servants in Germany by a ratio of 7:1 (United Nations Online Network in Public Administration and Finance); in Canada, the ratio of provincial to federal public servants in 2000 was less than 4:1 (Canadian Tax Foundation, Finances of the Nation, 2001). As we enter the new millennium in the United States, today there are approximately 2.9 million civilian employees of the federal government and approximately 16 million state and local civil servants.

3.4.3 FISCAL POWERS

As each of us is aware from time to time, governments do more than make and enforce laws; they also (or as a result of legislation) spend money through programs, and collect taxes to fund their expenditures. The term "fiscal" directs our attention to the revenues and spending of governments. Just as the autonomy we associate with genuine federalism requires that each level of government be able to make laws in some areas without the consent of the other level of government, so, too, we might argue, federalism requires that each government have the authority to raise the revenues necessary to finance its expenditures. In the best of all possible worlds each government's revenue capacity (which is not the same as its revenue authority) will match its expenditure needs, but in the real world, for many reasons, an **IMBALANCE** occurs. In some cases the constitution may allocate revenue sources (e.g., types of taxation) unequally between the levels of state, perhaps reflecting a judgment of unequal need. In 1980 the United States government funded 23 per cent of the expenditures of local and state governments (Janda, Berry, and Goldman, 1989: 121); today, this figure has risen slightly to more than 25 per cent. The amount of money being transferred is substantial. Despite the attempts of the Reagan administration to cut back on federal subsidies to other government levels in the 1980s, these payments still amount to about $250 billion a year (1997 figures, and the trend is upward). Other countries' experience with intergovernmental transfer payments varies. In 1999-2000, 34.6 per cent of Australian states' revenue came from the federal government (down from almost 60 per cent in the early 1990s), and in Canada in 2000, federal transfers accounted for 13.5 per cent of provincial revenue (Australian Yearbook 2002; Canadian Tax Foundation, Finances of the Nation, 2001). Obviously, the more financially autonomous the various levels of government are, the more opportunity they have to behave independently.

The means by which fiscal **TRANSFERS** are made from one level to another are various. One useful distinction is between *general purpose* and *specific purpose* transfers, the former being transfers to the general revenue of the recipient government, the latter (called "grants-in-aid" in the U.S.) being monies targeted for specific programs or program areas. The bulk of transfers from the federal government come in the form of specific purpose transfers, which normally (but not always) go to the individual states and municipalities on an equal per capita basis. Here, too, it is useful to distinguish between *categorical* grants and *block* grants, the former being funds to be spent in a particular area meeting a more or less stringent set of federally set conditions, the latter being monies intended for expenditure in particular policy areas, but over which the recipient governments exercise complete control. About 10 per cent of all federal aid to state and local governments has been in the form of block grants. This practice had been declining through the 1980s, but beginning in 1995 the flow of federal aid funds from the federal to state and local governments through these grants began to increase, as a result of the new Republican majority in Congress wishing to transfer welfare spending (in particular) to locally administered programs.

Approximately 90 per cent of all federal transfer payments to subnational levels of government come in the form of categorical grants. As noted, these grants are a means by which the federal government gains policy leverage in a field in which it has no constitutional legislative competence. For example, the availability of national aid for elementary and secondary education beginning in 1965 was a powerful incentive for communities to desegregate their educational system. And during the energy crisis of the 1970s, federal highway assistance to states was made conditional on the adoption of a 55-mile-per-hour speed limit. All states did so (though this requirement was repealed finally in 1995). Similarly, in 2001 the *No Child Left Behind Act* aimed to close the achievement gap between disadvantaged and minority students and their peers. In the process, it encouraged the spread of competency testing in school systems throughout the country.

Discussion of the **DIVISION OF POWERS** directs our attention to federalism as a relationship between governments, federal and regional. Yet, as we have seen, an underlying rationale for having two levels of government may well be to represent different populations or cultures traditionally identified with the territorial subunits. Representing the people in two different dimensions, national and subnational, can be accomplished, then, through having two levels of government, one corresponding to each dimension of society. It is also possible to represent the two dimensions of society within the national government, and this is the function of a bicameral legislature and more specifically of the second chamber of a **BICAMERAL** legislature in federal systems. In other words, in a federal polity, the second (or "upper") chamber of the legislature represents in some way the people or governments of the subnational or regional states.

In most bicameral democracies, the lower chamber, the one to which the government is responsible, is elected on the principle of *representation by population*, sometimes articulated as "one person, one vote." If consistently adhered to, this principle will give the people *of the country* equal representation in the legislative chamber: each citizen's vote will carry the same weight. This also means that more populous regions or federal units will have a greater number of representatives than less populous areas. In the United States, after the 2000 census California had 53 representatives in the House of Representatives, while seven states had just one. In federal countries, then, the second chamber will serve to represent the regional or subnational units in some way. (This is what Lijphart calls "incongruence," the two chambers of the legislature are constituted on distinct bases, i.e., represent wholly different constituencies.)

The simplest way to do this is give an equal number of seats to each unit. Thus, in the United States each state elects two senators to the Senate, regardless of state population. In Germany, by contrast, each *Land* is represented in the *Bundesrat* by 3, 4, or 5 votes, depending on its population, and the members of the *Bundesrat* are appointed by the *Land* governments, which means that this chamber is in fact a federal council representing the governments of the *Länder*, rather than a legislative chamber representing constituencies. Within federal democracies, the Canadian Senate is something of an anomaly. First of all, the Canadian Senate is a patronage chamber: the Senators are chosen by the Prime Minister and tend to be party members rewarded for loyal service. Senators serve until age 75, regardless of whether they are active in their service. This non-democratic appointment system deprives

**3.5
Bicameralism in
Federal States**

the Canadian Senate of legitimacy, and ensures its subordination to the democratically elected House of Commons. Second, the Canadian Senate represents regions rather than provinces: prior to the incorporation of Newfoundland as the tenth province (with 6 Senate seats) in 1949, there were four regions with 24 Senators each (Atlantic Canada, Quebec, Ontario, and the West), plus one for each of the Territories. This creates a very unequal representation in provincial terms, and one that satisfies almost no one.

As important as the basis of representation in second chambers, and often related to it, is the power of the second chamber relative to the first or lower house. In parliamentary systems, normally the second chamber cannot bring down the government; the first chamber is the *confidence chamber*. For this reason, there is often a requirement that bills (i.e., legislative proposals) involving the expenditure of money be introduced in the first chamber, although this is also required in the U.S. Congress, which has no rules of confidence. The key issue here is whether or not the second chamber has the ability to veto or block legislation coming from the lower house. There is a strong argument to be made that second chambers, which represent the regional states, must have some such ability if they are to represent their constituencies effectively in the national government. This is what Lijphart calls **SYMMETRY** between the chambers of the legislature, and the combination of incongruence and symmetry creates what he calls strong bicameralism. In other words, under such conditions, the two houses of the legislature have a relatively equal weight in the legislative process, or conversely, the upper house does not simply give formal approval to what emerges from the lower chamber. Of the five federal systems included in his study of 21 democracies, Lijphart concludes that four (Australia, Germany, Switzerland, and the United States) qualify as strongly bicameral; the one which does not is Canada (1984: 99).

It is important to remember that the ability of the upper chamber to defeat or block legislation from the lower chamber must be matched by a willingness to do so. If party discipline is weak, then such a possibility is more or less continuous. The United States Congress provides perhaps the clearest example of two legislative chambers with more or less equal weight in the legislative process, so much so that most bills move through the two houses simultaneously, rather than sequentially, as is the parliamentary norm. A bill may survive either or neither chamber, but then again, bills in this system are not "government" bills and their fate has no bearing on the term of the political executive. In parliamentary systems, where the requirements of responsible government have produced strong parties, the conditions of strong bicameralism will tend to come into play only if the party or parties controlling the government are in a minority in the upper chamber. In such a case, "the opposition" controls the second chamber.

To contrast with American bicameralism, then, in parliamentary Australia most legislation is government legislation, and any defeat presents implications (if not indications) of non-confidence. In 1975, the opposition controlled the Australian Senate, and refused passage to the Labour government's appropriations bills (which authorize government expenditures) when they were received from the lower chamber. In the view of the opposition, this constituted a vote of non-confidence in the government, whose resignation it demanded. The Prime Minister and his party argued that parliamentary government requires the confidence of the lower chamber only, a position that is true by convention in some democracies, and constitutionally established in others. On the other hand, a government that cannot get parliamentary authorization for its expenditures is a government that cannot govern. In a move that remains controversial, the Governor-General dismissed the Labour government and ordered new elections for both houses of the Australian parliament, elections won by the opposition Liberal-National coalition. Significantly, it is the incongruence of the two chambers in a federal system that leads to the possibility that the majority in either chamber could be controlled by a different party or group of parties, something made more likely when elections for the chambers take place at different times.

Part of the difficulty in the Australian case was the lack of clarity concerning the significance of a defeat in the second chamber for the survival of the government. Such a problem does not exist in Germany. Constitutionally, only the lower or first chamber (the *Bundestag*) can defeat the government, so any defeat of legislation by the second chamber (the *Bundesrat*) is simply that. In addition, the veto exercised by the *Bundesrat* is qualified: it is an absolute veto only on matters that touch upon the interests of the *Länder*. On all other matters, the lower house may override the veto of the upper chamber with a second vote of its own. This means that on non-*Länder* issues, the veto of the second house is a very limited **SUSPENSIVE VETO**. Such a device gives second chambers power, but not the ultimate ability to thwart the government.

This inability of a second chamber to stymie a government is particularly attractive in systems where the second chamber lacks the democratic legitimacy of the first or popularly elected chamber.

In (non-federal) Britain, for example, the House of Lords is a remnant of the days of feudal aristocracy, being composed of a mixture of hereditary and life (appointed) peers. Such a representation of class and privilege is difficult to reconcile with the norms of democracy and egalitarianism that have been proclaimed (if not fully realized) in the twentieth century, and not surprisingly is unique to Britain. At any rate, since 1911, the House of Lords has had only a suspensive veto over legislation, and in 1949 the length of that suspensive period was reduced from two years to one. The idea of reforming the Lords has been around for a long time. Traditionally in favor of the abolition of the second chamber, the currently governing Labour Party moderated its stance in the early 1990s instead to advocate a two-stage reform process. In 1999, Tony Blair's Labour government introduced the House of Lords Bill, which would have removed all seats for hereditary peers. In order to speed passage of the bill in the face of opposition from the Conservative-dominated life peers, the government agreed to a compromise in which 92 seats would be retained for hereditary peers, at least until a second round of reforms is undertaken (to come after a Royal Commission has reported on ways to modernize the structure) (see Figure 3.3 for a comparison of the composition of the Lords before and after the Blair government reforms). As it stands now, however, the reformed Lords has eliminated some of the most egregious vestiges of aristocratic privilege in the British system.

REFORMING THE BRITISH HOUSE OF LORDS

	COMPOSITION IN 1999 (pre-reform)	COMPOSITION IN 2002 (post-reform)
Archbishops & Bishops	26	26
Life Peers (appointed)	485	585
Hereditary Peers	759	91
Total	1,270	702

FIGURE 3.3

Canada's upper chamber represents an unsatisfactory compromise between the British second chamber and the American Senate, which represents the regional units of state (the federal function). It has been pointed out that Canada's Senate was designed as a chamber of "sober second thought" in order to protect the interests of property against possible incursions by the policies of a popularly elected (and therefore intemperate) lower house. For that reason, Canadian Senators were, and remain, appointed by the Governor-General on the advice of the Prime Minister. Such an appointed body offends the principles of democracy (see Figure 3.3), but it also fails to perform the federal function of a second chamber adequately, because the Prime Minister's appointees can hardly be said to represent either the provincial populations or the provincial governments.

One consequence of the lack of perceived legitimacy of the Senate is that Canada has not faced a crisis such as the Australian situation of 1975. The rare instances when the Senate defeats legislation coming from the House of Commons are not seen to have implications of confidence, and the Senate seems to have avoided defeating any legislation that might be seen to have such an import. A more subtle tactic is to amend legislation and send it back to the House of Commons. If such legislation comes back a second time in its original form, the senators are likely to give it reluctant passage. Not surprisingly, there has been no shortage of calls to reform the Canadian Senate, and most focus on improving its capability of representing the provinces (their peoples, or their governments). It is difficult to argue with the proposition that if the Senate cannot perform the function of representing the provinces adequately, it has no reason for existing.

In the preceding sections we have employed a fairly orthodox definition of federalism which insists that the two levels of government—national and regional—must be autonomous of each other, and we have indicated several ways in which this can be true. In this section we want to consider several situations that do not satisfy the strict definition of federalism, but that have a similar effect or may accomplish the same purposes as federalism.

3.6
Home Rule and Decentralization in Unitary States

HOME RULE is another concept closely related to federalism and exists when a territory or region within a unitary state achieves autonomy or special status. In other words, a particular government exists in this region, but not others. The obvious basis for such an **ASYMMETRICAL FEDERALISM** is clearly cultural, focusing on a minority language, ethnicity, and/or religion. Britain is a unitary state, but there has been much discussion lately about the prospects for some measure of home rule for the country's predominantly Celtic peripheries. When the Welsh overwhelmingly rejected the question in a 1979 referendum, a majority of those voting in Scotland were in favor—but the turnout was too low for the result to count. The Labour Party that came to power in the summer of 1997 did so after campaigning in favor of **DEVOLUTION** for Scotland and Wales. Devolution in this context involved transferring powers and a measure of self-government to Scottish and Welsh parliaments. As a result of this campaign promise, Prime Minister Tony Blair's government held referendums in both regions. Scotland voted strongly in favor of a separate Scottish Parliament to be created in Edinburgh on September 11, 1997; one week later a narrow majority of Welsh residents voted in favor of a Welsh Assembly (see Figure 3.4). The Assemblies that were put in place as a result of these votes are quite different, however. The Scottish Parliament is able to overturn U.K. legislation, raise its own finances through taxation, and introduce bills in areas not retained by the national Parliament in Westminster. The Welsh Assembly, on the other hand, can only amend Westminster legislation in areas specifically devolved to it, and it relies solely on money transferred from London. As a result, the Scottish Parliament has far greater home rule power than the Welsh Assembly.

As extensive as the home rule provisions in the United Kingdom are, however, it is worth remembering that these two assemblies exist "at the pleasure" of the central government of the United Kingdom; it is not inconceivable that they might be disbanded at some future point, should the central government so desire. Other European unitary states have also devolved some autonomy to distinctive regions. The Finnish island of Åland, which has a large Swedish-speaking population, has extensive autonomy or home rule, including a parliament with powers over health policy, education, and environmental policy (Lane and Ersson, 1991: 219). In Denmark, the Faroe Islands and Greenland each have their own legislature and executive.

Finally, we should note the trend within even centralized unitary states for a wholesale decentralization of power. This normally results when a whole new level of regional government is created. In some cases this is the result of ideology, but there is a strongly pragmatic basis to decentralization: as the size and extent of the state have grown, it has become more difficult or inefficient to try to govern from one center. Decentralization often entails establishing administrative districts and corresponding offices for the purposes of administering the programs and enforcing the laws made by the national government. In this sense the state is decentralized but not the government as there are no regional legislatures or separate structures of representation. Decentralization of the administrative or bureaucratic apparatus can also provide a basis, though, for the development of autonomy in other ways. Spain, constitutionally a unitary state, has for many years endured nationalist or separatist pressures from various ethnic divisions, and in some regions (most

DEVOLUTION REFERENDA IN SCOTLAND AND WALES

SCOTLAND	1979	1997
% of those voting in favor of a separate assembly	52	74
% Turnout	33	60
WALES		
% of those voting in favor of a separate assembly	20	50
% Turnout	59	50

FIGURE 3.4

notably the Basque) there has been terrorism and violence. The response of the Spanish government has been to create a system of regional governments, and in areas where unrest has been greatest, to negotiate considerable **AUTONOMY** for the regional governments. Spain now has a system of 17 autonomous regional governments, each with its own executive and legislature, but the powers enjoyed by each depends on agreements negotiated with the Spanish state. Four of the most nationalist regions—Catalonia, the Basque Country, Galicia, and Andalusia—have achieved a considerable degree of autonomy. Thus, although Spain is not strictly speaking a federal system, it contains considerable degrees of asymmetrical regional autonomy, attaining in some cases what might be considered home rule.

In the 1970s and 1980s two other highly centralized states, Italy and France, each established new tiers of regional governments. In Italy, five of the 20 Italian regions created were given **SPECIAL AUTONOMY** to reflect the cultural and ethnic distinctiveness of particular border regions where there had been some separatist sentiment at the end of World War II. These regional governments are democratically elected and they exercise a wide range of powers. Still other mechanisms may be found to decentralize power in unitary states. In the Scandinavian countries, for example, decentralization has been achieved not by creating regional governments, but by delegating to and increasing the autonomy of local governments.

3.7 Supranational Federalism: The European Union

In the second half of the twentieth century, the emergence and development of the **EUROPEAN UNION** demonstrated the possibility that federalism cannot arise only within a nation state (e.g., Belgium), or through the union of what had been colonies into a state (e.g., the U.S. or Canada), but also serve as a system for governing associated sovereign nation-states. What began as a limited trade association among six nations (the European Coal and Steel Community, created in 1951) became a commitment to the creation of a common market and united policies on matters such as transportation and agriculture (the European Economic Community, created in 1957). Most recently, the scope of the European Union's authority has extended with the introduction of a common currency (adopted by most of its member states), customs union, and even defense and foreign policy. Along with this expansion of functions has come a broadening of membership, from the original six countries (France, Germany, Italy, Belgium,

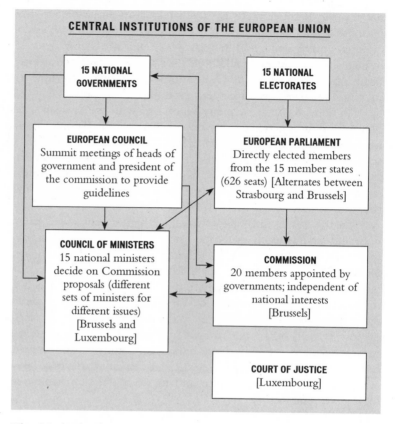

CENTRAL INSTITUTIONS OF THE EUROPEAN UNION

15 NATIONAL GOVERNMENTS

15 NATIONAL ELECTORATES

EUROPEAN COUNCIL
Summit meetings of heads of government and president of the commission to provide guidelines

EUROPEAN PARLIAMENT
Directly elected members from the 15 member states (626 seats) [Alternates between Strasbourg and Brussels]

COUNCIL OF MINISTERS
15 national ministers decide on Commission proposals (different sets of ministers for different issues) [Brussels and Luxembourg]

COMMISSION
20 members appointed by governments; independent of national interests [Brussels]

COURT OF JUSTICE
[Luxembourg]

FIGURE 3.5

The Netherlands, and Luxembourg) to nine countries in 1973 (adding Britain, Denmark, and Ireland), to 12 in the mid-1980s (with the addition of Greece, Spain, and Portugal), to its current 15 member states (when Austria, Finland, and Sweden joined in 1995). In late 2002, the European Commission recommended that the eight former Soviet bloc countries (the Czech Republic, Estonia, Hungary, Latvia, Lithuania, Poland, Slovakia, and Slovenia) along with Malta and Cyprus be admitted to full membership in 2004, Bulgaria and Romania in 2007. Currently, there are more than 375 million citizens of the EU, making this a formidable force in the contemporary world. This is an extraordinary set of developments on a continent that was twice the focal point of World Wars within the last century.

As the scope of the European Union has enlarged and as expansion of membership has accelerated, questions have been raised about the present and future governance of the Union. At present, the governing structure of the EU looks like that of no other political system we have discussed. There are four main political institutions, as well as a Court of Justice. The complexity of the relationship among these units is clear from Figure 3.5.

Taken together, they define a complete and increasingly autonomous political system at the European level. As time passes, the EU operates more and more like a state, giving rise in some quarters to fears of an emergent European "superstate." Citizens in many countries carry EU currency in their pockets, travel abroad using burgundy EU passports, and enjoy freedom of movement across member state borders.

The legislative branch (the European Parliament) is directly elected by citizens in member states across Europe in elections held every five years. The 626 seats in the European Parliament are apportioned among the member states according to population, but smaller states are over-represented in relation to larger ones. The powers of the Parliament depend on the subject being considered. Although much of its work is advisory to other EU bodies, the Parliament's immediate mandate has expanded in recent years, particularly in terms of budgetary and executive oversight and concerning the accession of new member states.

The European Commission, which is both similar to and different from a cabinet, consists of 20 members appointed by the member states, normally after they have completed a distinguished career in domestic politics. Each individual member assumes a portfolio consisting of a field of policy. These individuals swear an oath promising to pursue European and not narrow national interests in the discharge of their duties. The Commission must be approved by Parliament before it takes office. Although the Commission is responsible for initiating legislation, its proposals may be overruled by the Council (see below) and it may be requested by the Council to draft proposals on a particular subject. Similarly, while the Commission is the body that monitors compliance by member states with EU policies, its ability to enforce implementation is weak. The authority of the Commission suffered greatly in 1999; as a result of widespread financial scandals and allegations of corruption, it was forced to resign by the European Parliament.

The most powerful body with respect to policy-making in the EU is the Council of Ministers, which represents the governments of the member states. Each country's seat is filled by a minister from its government. Which minister attends a Council meeting depends on the topic under discussion. One meeting might bring together all transportation ministers of member states to discuss trucking regulations; another might involve all health

KEY TERMS

asymmetrical federalism
autonomy
bicameralism
confederation
concurrency
congruence
decentralization
delegation
devolution
division of powers
European Union
federalism
fiscal imbalance
home rule
jurisdiction
paramountcy
quasi-federal
residual clause
special autonomy
supranational federalism
suspensive veto
symmetry
transfers
unitary state

ministers considering home-care standards. On all issues except the EU's budget, the Council is the final step in the decision-making process. Whereas the early decades saw each member of the Council wield a veto, more recent years have seen the emergence and spread of "qualified majority voting." The most important topics are reserved for meetings of the heads of state/government (Prime Ministers and Presidents) and these are known as "European Council" meetings. Now European Council meetings are carefully prepared and closely watched as leaders plot the future of this extraordinary emergent political system.

As the above brief description of EU institutions implies, the organization is closer to a confederation than a federation, in that member states have surrendered very little of their national sovereignty to the larger body, and each is free to withdraw from the Union at any time. Many of the issues critical to the future of the EU—from further economic and political integration, to expansion to Eastern Europe, to the establishment of a European defense force—will hinge on whether or not the member states will surrender more authority to the Union's institutions. As the failure of all members to agree to the adoption of common borders and the Euro (the EU currency) shows, getting all 15 to move at the same speed towards closer integration is a tall order. However, one must be impressed with the remarkable progress that has been made towards the establishment of a common political association in a part of the world better known for its conflictual past than its record of co-operation.

What all of the examples in this section demonstrate is that while the number of countries that qualify as federal may be few when the definitions are strictly applied, there are any number of ways in which political systems may incorporate elements of federalism, or apply federal solutions to their problems without actually adopting federalism. It is our hunch, moreover, that, formally or informally, federalism is something the world's citizens are going to see more of in the coming decades.

REFERENCES AND SUGGESTED READING

Burgess, Michael, and Alain-G. Gagnon. 1993. *Comparative Federalism and Federation.* Toronto: University of Toronto Press.

Elazar, Daniel. 1987. *Exploring Federalism.* Tuscaloosa: University of Alabama Press.

Lane, Jan-Erik, and Svante O. Ersson. 1991. *Politics and Society in Western Europe.* Beverly Hills, CA: Sage Publications.

Lijphart, Arend. 1984. *Democracies: Patterns of Majoritarian and Consensus Government in Twenty-One Countries.* New Haven: Yale University Press.

Mahler, Gregory. 1995. *Comparative Politics: An Institutional and Cross-National Approach.* Englewood Cliffs, NJ: Prentice-Hall.

Mény, Yves. 1993. *Government and Politics in Western Europe*, 2nd ed. Oxford: Oxford University Press.

Nugent, Neill. 2003. *Government and Politics of the European Union*, 5th ed. New York: Palgrave.

Stanley, Harold, and Richard Niemi. 1994. *Vital Statistics on American Politics*, 4th ed. Washington: CQ Press.

Stevenson, Garth. 1989. *Unfulfilled Union: Canadian Federalism and National Unity.* 3rd ed. Toronto: Gage.

Wheare, K.C. 1963. *Federal Government.* London: Oxford University Press.

FOUR | Cleavage Structures and Electoral Systems

How can one conceive of a one-party system in a country that has over 200 varieties of cheeses?

— Charles de Gaulle

In this chapter we will look at the divisions that give rise to the conflict and competition so necessary to the vitality of liberal democracy. With an understanding of the ways in which social divisions can be seen to structure political competition, we then turn to the rules governing the conduct of elections.

One of the recurring themes in definitions of politics is the resolution of conflict, and we might well ask, conflict between whom, and over what? Part of the answer is contained in our observation about the character of most modern societies: they are pluralistic aggregations of several or many communities—their identity is multiple. The conflict states must resolve is sometimes a dispute between individuals, but it is as often, and perhaps more importantly, about competition between different segments of society, and it is competition for influence, if not control, over the policy outputs that government delivers. In turning to cleavages in this chapter, we are looking at the bases of division within a society, the societal sources of the peaceful competition and conflict that is resolved through the political process.

The fundamental nature of these divisions is recognized by Lane and Ersson when they describe cleavages

4.1 Cleavages Defined

4.1 Cleavages Defined
4.2 Some Cleavages Examined
    4.2.1 Religious
    4.2.2 Ethno-Linguistic
    4.2.3 Center-Periphery
    4.2.4 Urban-Rural
    4.2.5 Class
4.3 Reinforcing and Cross-Cutting Cleavages
4.4 Electoral Systems: The Basics
4.5 Electoral Systems: Main Variants
    4.5.1 Single-Member (Majoritarian) Systems
    4.5.2 Proportionate Electoral Systems
    4.5.3 Hybrid (Mixed-Member) Systems
4.6 Party Systems
4.7 Conclusion

as "the so-called raw materials of politics which political parties mold by aligning themselves in a party system facing the electorate in competitive elections. Public institutions offer decision-making mechanisms for handling issues that somehow relate to the cleavages in the social structure" (1991: 11). Similarly, Gallagher et al. describe cleavages as "the actual substance of the social divisions that underpin contemporary ... politics" (1992: 210).

Building on the work of Lipset and Rokkan (1967), Gallagher et al. suggest that a cleavage involves three dimensions:

1. a "social division" between people in terms of some central characteristic,

2. a collective identification in terms of this social division, and

3. some organization that gives "institutional expression" to this collective identification (1992: 210-11).

Each of these points deserves expansion. The first suggests that not only do people identify themselves in terms of a common characteristic, but also that this is a basis for distinguishing themselves from others who do not share in this defining criterion. There are, in fact, many different bases on which such divisions may rest, but the most compelling are those that turn out to be, at least in some degree, **ASCRIPTIVE VARIABLES**. By this term we would designate characteristics that are somehow innate (race), or inherited (mother tongue), or (for at least one's formative years) involuntarily assigned (religion, class). This allows us to distinguish the identities on which cleavages rest from those identities or identifications that are more consciously selected or manufactured, such as an ideology, or a political party, or an interest group. Each of these latter may, in fact, be linked very closely to a cleavage (e.g., socialism and class; Christian Democratic parties and religion), but need not necessarily be so connected.

The second element of cleavages also indicates how the distinction we have just made is not entirely artificial. You could hardly belong to a political party or an interest group without being aware of or identifying yourself as a member of these organizations. It is entirely possible, if not in fact often the case, that we do *not* identify ourselves in terms of our race, or mother tongue, or class. We each have racial or ethnic, linguistic, and class characteristics, but may not see these as the things that determine who we are and what we want. Very often these characteristics become "visible" to us only in the presence of others, whose characteristics are different. In this sense, a cleavage does not rest on the fact of difference, but on the *perception* of difference.

Third, the perception of difference is by itself not enough to make a cleavage politically relevant. The collective identification of people in terms of their common characteristic must lead to some political action, and this will in all likelihood express itself in some form of organization. This is where cleavages may link up with ideology, or political parties or interest groups. Hence members of the working class, conscious of their collective identity and interest, may adopt a socialist ideology, establish trade unions, support the Social Democratic party, etc. The careful reader will have noticed that something extra slipped into that last sentence, namely the addition "and interest." We need this, or something like this, to explain how we get from consciousness of our identity in terms of a social characteristic, to organization for political action on the basis of this identity. To be conscious of my religious or ethnic or class identity has no political significance unless it also means that I have an interest that is connected to that identity, and that this interest is not being met, or is threatened, or requires protection, by the government. The division at the basis of a cleavage must be not simply a difference in identities, but a *difference in interests*, where interest directs us to what a group (or individual for that matter) wants or believes it needs. Its political interests will be receiving the public policies that it wants or needs, and enduring none that are contrary to its wants or needs. In our view it is a difference in interest (real or perceived) that is critical to the movement from collective identity to organization for political action. This is the difference between cleavages that remain latent, and those that become manifest in the body politic. This may become clearer if we look at some of the more common cleavages within modern societies.

At the risk of oversimplification, cleavages are the product of history: either significant changes in the nature of a society (a religious schism, the emergence of a new economic system, the impact of technology, etc.) have conspired to differentiate its people on a fresh basis; or wars, conquests, or political union have put together different peoples into one society. By and large either or both of these are true of the cleavages considered below.

**4.2
Some Cleavages Examined**

4.2.1 RELIGIOUS

One of the oldest cleavages in most Western democracies, and one which had much to do with the emergence of modern society in Western Europe and its dependencies, is that presented by **RELIGIOUS DIFFERENCE**. This is also a cleavage that can most seriously threaten the peace and stability of a society. The Reformation in Europe led to, or served as an excuse for, any number of civil wars and wars between nation-states. Interestingly, even today most European countries remain overwhelmingly Catholic or Protestant, and it is not an exaggeration to say that in most of the world still, religious pluralism either is unknown or is a source of tension. One need only think of the world's persistent trouble spots to identify clashes which are based, in whole or in part, on religious difference: Bosnia, Northern Ireland, Cyprus, Kashmir, Lebanon, etc. In countries where religious differences have remained at worst matters of civil conflict, the political questions have focused on the role of the state in protecting a religion's values or traditional practices. For a variety of historical reasons, countries where there is a strict constitutional separation of church and state as in the United States have been rare. If not constitutionally, then in practice, or perhaps traditionally in past practice, the state has tended to favor one religion or another in some of its policies, and this creates resentment or demand for equity from other religious denominations. In some European countries (and among some of the Christian right in the U.S.) the religious cleavage is not so much interdenominational, but between those who continue to defend a wholly secular state, and those who would make religious values once again part of official decision-making, or seek to make pubic policy consistent with church teachings. We should perhaps also note that in talking about the religious cleavage we are talking as much (if not more) about a social identification than about any commitment to a particular spirituality. In many cases the conflict between adherents of rival creeds has little to do with theology or devotion, and everything to do with a way of life and identification within the community. In plural, secular North American society, religious belief and practice is often seen to be simply a matter of personal choice; in many other societies religious affiliation has a much more collective and social character: religion cannot be so simply or neatly extricated from other aspects of life.

4.2.2 ETHNO-LINGUISTIC

A variety of different but similar variables can be treated here. Despite the increasing doubts that scientists have with the concept of **RACE**, we can easily note the existence of many societies in which race has been (Uganda) and/or remains a significant cleavage (the U.S., South Africa, Malaysia). Most of these cleavages are the unhappy legacy of colonialism and imperialism. In many other cases, though, political union or conquests or dynastic marriages have joined different **ETHNIC** and **LINGUISTIC** communities (which are not so distinct racially) in one society. English and French in Canada; Flemish and Walloon in Belgium; or French, German, and Italian in Switzerland are more striking examples of advanced democracies with a significant ethno-linguistic cleavage, but countries like Spain, France, and Britain also score high on indices of ethnic diversity (see Lane and Ersson, 1991: 75). It is important to understand that these cleavages are never just about language, but also about cultural differences rooted in or sustained through linguistic difference. In some cases, like the Scottish or Welsh in Britain, the cultural differences may in fact have survived the demise or decline of the native tongue. As we will discuss shortly, such ethno-linguistic cleavage seems rarely to exist in isolation, but is rather often linked to another, such as religion or **CLASS**. In and of itself, the ethno-linguistic cleavage mobilizes its supporters around issues relevant to the survival of the culture: measures protecting and preserving use of the language, education, and other cultural supports. In some cases freedom from discrimination, or redress for historic injustices will also be high on the agenda. Most important is some kind of political power with which to guarantee favorable policies. For political majorities this is not a problem; ethno-linguistic minorities, though, will seek some manner of constitutional protection, special representation, and/or autonomy within the system.

4.2.3 CENTER-PERIPHERY

This cleavage is a function of size (i.e., **POPULATION**) and distance (i.e., geography), in that without a significant separation of population there can, by definition, be no center and periphery, but there is more to it than this. As in all other cleavages, the difference *has to matter* in some way. Virtually all societies—city-states or micro-states excepted—will have a center, and what makes it the center is not its location but its *centrality* within the society. It is the largest city or most populous region, it may be the political capital, and/or the most economically developed and productive region. In most cases, then, this centrality will be a source of resentment to regions or areas that feel disadvantaged or excluded by not being at the center. "**METROPOLE**" and "**HINTERLAND**" is another way of characterizing the halves of this cleavage, which is apt in that hinterland has the connotation of a region exploited or used for the benefit of the metropole, something that is very likely to cause resentment among those who inhabit the hinterland. In the northern provinces of Italy in the 1990s, growth in support for political movements with separatist agendas (regional leagues) pointed in a more disruptive direction. Italy is governed from Rome, which is situated in the more populous, but also poorer, southern half of the country. As in most modern countries, the Italian state performs a redistributive function, which in this case means that the industrialized urban north subsidizes the more rural, poorer south. Northern support for separatist parties means a wealthy hinterland seeking to be free from a needy metropole.

To a considerable degree, the center-periphery cleavage accounts for what is commonly called "**POLITICAL REGIONALISM**," which exists whenever the identification with a particular territory within a larger geographic whole becomes a factor in political activity. By itself, though, identification with a particular territorial region will not provide the basis for political action; something else must unite and motivate the people within this region. Our neighbor to the north exhibits a pattern of regional politics that illustrates the significance of more than one cleavage. There are many cases then, where regionalism reflects, as it does in Western Canada, primarily a center-periphery cleavage, but there are other cases, such as in the Province of Quebec, where regionalism is based on another cleavage or cleavages (in this case primarily ethno-linguistic and social-economic divisions).

4.2.4 URBAN-RURAL

The urban-rural cleavage illustrates an important point, namely that for a cleavage to play a significant role in a country's politics, there must be some measure of balance between the two sides of the division. To speak of an urban-rural cleavage in the middle ages, when there were few cities, would be rather silly, but the same is just as true in many parts of the industrialized world today where more than 80 per cent of the population lives in cities. This doesn't mean that there isn't a contrast and often a conflict of interest between those who live in the cities and those who still live in the country. Indeed, rural Americans tend to be more socially conservative than their urban counterparts, and thus appeals by politicians and parties to "family values" tend to resonate more strongly in rural areas. Similarly, opposition to gun control is strongest in rural America. Access to quality health care, Internet communications infrastructure, and some government programs are other concerns disproportionately felt by residents of rural areas. Some have argued that these issues are driving a resurgence of rural-urban conflict in the United States (and in other countries), but the balance of power is so clearly held by urban dwellers that the cleavage is probably less significant than it once was. It may well be that in many places the urban-suburban cleavage is as relevant as the urban-rural once was.

4.2.5 CLASS

There are several compelling reasons for arguing that **CLASS** has become the most significant of the cleavages in contemporary politics, and most observers would agree with Gallagher et al. that this has been especially true of Western European politics (1992: 214). It is even possible to see the rural-urban cleavage, in many cases, as rooted in class differences. Certainly all countries are not characterized by ethno-linguistic difference, or religious distinctions, or center-periphery conflicts, but all have economic classes. Two factors must be kept in mind here: *how* we define and identify class, and that class, like other bases of identity, may remain a *latent* cleavage in some systems.

Class, in any society, represents social stratifications that give differential access to resources and other societal goods. How these classes are to be defined and identified depends, in part, on perspective. Marx, for example, defined classes *structurally*, in terms of the organization of the means of economic production in any society, and believed that the capitalist mode of production created essentially two classes: owners and workers. For Marx, modern politics would be the class struggle between these two classes (and eventually the victory of the working class). In fact, in modern industrial (or now post-industrial) economies, the structure of capitalism is much more complex. In addition to owners and workers there are considerable numbers who are neither: the self-employed (who Marx thought would be insignificant), the unemployed, those employed in public or quasi-public institutions, farmers, students, etc. Division *within* classes, or class fractions, can be as significant as the divisions between classes. Different segments of the business community have different needs and interests, above and beyond what they share in common. Similarly, workers of blue, white, and pink collars may as much be in competition and conflict with each other as with their bosses. An increasing fragmentation of the classes, considered structurally, puts impediments in the way of class politics. Sociologically, class is more likely to be considered today in terms of measures such as income, education, status, or composites that combine several of these. To the extent that class becomes an academic construct it is less likely to form the basis of an identity on which a politics will be based.

It is possible that however real class may be, it remains a **LATENT CLEAVAGE**, and there are several reasons for this. One is the growth of a so-called middle-class society in the affluent world, combined with the strength of those ideologies and cultural beliefs that ignore or minimize the significance of class in such societies. Studies show that the overwhelming majority view themselves as members of the middle class, which may reflect in part the structural fragmentation noted above, as well as the relative affluence of all in these societies. It also means almost automatically that they cannot conceive of class as the basis on which their politics needs to be based. As with all cleavages, there must be a significant "other" or the **BASIS OF IDENTITY** does not become politicized. In societies where there are strong cultural beliefs that argue (contrary to all evidence) that individuals' social positions are the product of their hard work, intelligence, and initiative, to be disadvantaged in class terms can be a sign of failure. Certainly, in most European democracies, class is a significant cleavage, but it is much less so in North America, where political parties that campaign on behalf of a particular class are rare, and rarely successful. This is not to say that class is not an important variable in North American politics, only that it is not the primary identity that informs the political consciousness and action of large segments of society.

Any society will have a cleavage structure that will reflect some, but probably not all, of the cleavages discussed above. Across generations, the cleavages that matter politically may shift as technological, social, and demographic change work their effect. There may be other cleavages (like age) that remain latent but have the potential to manifest themselves at some future date. The constellation of cleavages that is operating in any given society has two significant relationships: one internal and one external. This latter is the relationship between the cleavages and the political organizations and institutions where behavior occurs. As noted, a cleavage may account for the support given to a political party, to an **INTEREST GROUP**, or to the strength of an ideology within a political culture. Political parties, interest groups, and any other vehicles of representation will succeed or fail to obtain policies that respond to the needs of the segments of society they represent. In this way cleavages are accommodated within the polity, or not. When a cleavage is most fully accommodated by responsive policies within a political community, the division represented by the cleavage ceases to be a basis for political mobilization. At worst, a cleavage that cannot be accommodated leads to civil war (see the former Yugoslavia) or partition (see the former Czechoslovakia) or other forms of extreme conflict. The ability of the society to accommodate or at least contain its cleavages will depend on features of the party system that we will be discussing below, in particular the electoral and party systems, which in turn shape the nature of party government. What also matters is the internal relationship, that of the cleavages to each other.

The crucial distinction here is between **REINFORCING** and **CROSS-CUTTING** cleavages. In the former case, two or more bases of identity (or difference) are shared by the same population. This means, in effect, that on virtually every issue, the lines of opposition will separate the same groups from each other. In Austria, the Catholic population has tended to be more bourgeois; the working-class is generally anti-clerical. This division led to a brief civil war in the 1930s. Even more strikingly, in Belgium, the Flemish (Dutch) population is largely Catholic and generally more affluent than the Walloons (francophone), who are more **SECULAR**. Tension between the two groups exists here on at least three levels, and the effect of such reinforcement in the Belgian case has been a steady decentralization of the political system. Generally speaking, we would expect reinforcing cleavages to lead, all else being equal, to fragmentation of the polity, as happened in the former countries of Czechoslovakia and Yugoslavia. At the very least, reinforcing cleavages will require a special effort by all parties to avoid destabilizing consequences.

The situation is easier where cleavages do not coincide so neatly. Consider a situation where there is a strong religious cleavage, and at the same time a strong class cleavage, but each class is divided equally among those who fall on either side of the religious divide. Here the cleavages offset each other perfectly: those who are united by religion are divided by economic class, and vice versa. On different issues the majority and minority groups will not be identical. The more cross-cutting cleavages there are, the more political majorities will be shifting and temporary, favoring or alienating no particular group on a regular basis. In this way, cross-cutting cleavages can be stabilizing in a pluralistic society.

Cleavages draw our attention to the fragmentation of identity and interest in modern societies. A central task for the political system of any such society is to contain or defuse the differences and contests of interest that emerge out of these various identities. This is perhaps the element of politics that is identified as the resolution of conflict, the engineering of consent, or the art of compromise. If one side of any division is always the "winner" in battles over policy, then the losing party will soon feel aggrieved, exploited, alienated. The long-term consequences of such an outcome are rarely good for a political community. What will make a big difference in determining whether such outcomes are likely is the capacity of the political process to provide representation to the various segments of society and in so doing provide a share in government and/or a voice in the policy-process. Some observers have pointed to the declining rates of electoral participation in the United States as indicative of a growing tendency among groups of citizens to perceive that the system is unwilling or unable to respond to their interests (Patterson, 2002). To explore this further means moving from cleavages to the representative vehicles such as parties, organized groups, etc. It is our contention, though, that the nature of parties is itself greatly effected by the electoral system in which parties compete, and by the party system that the electoral system in turn has a large part in shaping. It is these institutional systems, electoral and party, that we will now examine.

**4.4
Electoral Systems:
The Basics**

In the modern age, most democracy is representative democracy, a term we reserve for those systems in which citizens have the opportunity to vote for representatives in periodic, competitive elections. Here we will take a closer look at the institutional machinery of the electoral process, and its consequences for vehicles of representation in the political process. After examining some technical issues that must be addressed by all systems, we will turn to perhaps the most significant variable within any country's political process: namely, its **ELECTORAL SYSTEM**. The electoral system in turn has enormous influence on the party system that operates in a country. The electoral and party system will determine the kind of parliamentary system that tends to prevail (as discussed in Chapter 2), and also influence the other vehicles of representation to which citizens turn for political organization.

It is possible for officials from all three "branches" of government, or types of governmental institution, to be subject to periodic election. In practice, though, most electoral politics, particularly at the national level, concerns choosing representatives to sit in the legislature, and in some bicameral legislatures, in both houses of the parliament. The only other commonly elected post in national government is that of president, and this is true of strong presidents in systems characterized by what we called presidentialism, and in some cases of presidents who serve as formal heads of state in parliamentary regimes. In the remainder of this chapter our focus will be on the selection of representatives for the legislature, and, in most cases, will remain with the lower or first chamber of the legislature (because of its role as the confidence chamber in parliamentary systems).

With regard to the last point, we should note that while different principles of representation exist, all (to our knowledge) first chambers in bicameral systems and all unitary legislatures are based on the principle of **REPRESENTATION BY POPULATION**. This is also known as the "one (hu)man, one vote, one value" principle, which requires that each citizen's vote carry (at least roughly) the same weight as that of every other citizen. In practice this means that each member of the legislature should ideally represent the same number of citizens (constituents). Thus, the territorial **SIZE** of each representative's district or **CONSTITUENCY** should be determined by population, and each should contain the same population. We say "should" because populations do not remain static, but shift through growth and migration. Periodically, then, constituency boundaries must change to keep the weight of each citizen's voice in the political process equal. This is one reason why in most (if not all) democracies, a regular census is taken.

The expansion of the franchise to include all adult citizens in the United States was a long and complicated process. In the late 1700s, an estimated 23 per cent of the voting age population was eligible to cast a ballot. All property and religious requirements for the vote were dropped in all states except North Carolina and Virginia by 1829, resulting in universal white male suffrage by that time. American women, however, had to mount a long struggle and did not win the right to vote until 1920. The fifteenth Amendment to the Constitution (1870) formally enfranchised African-Americans, following the abolition of slavery that resulted from the Civil War. A variety of restrictive practices (poll taxes; literacy tests, etc.) persisted in many parts of the American south until the 1960s, however. These practices effectively disenfranchised the African-American population in that region. By the beginning of the 1970s all adult American citizens (with the exception of convicted felons and those in mental institutions) enjoyed the right to vote.

We should also note that the re-definition of constituency (or electoral **DISTRICT**) boundaries made necessary by demographic change provides an opportunity for any party that controls this process to maximize their own electoral chances in future elections. If in two adjacent constituencies, the government won one electoral district by a two-to-one majority and lost the other by a slim margin, the temptation will be great to readjust the boundaries so that both electoral districts contain a simple majority of loyal supporters. Conversely, one might wish to concentrate as many of one's opponents supporters in one electoral district as possible. These kinds of manipulations of electoral boundaries go by the name of **GERRYMANDERING**, an activity that has much more potential in **PLURALITY** than **PROPORTIONATE** electoral systems. To avoid gerrymandering, the business of adjusting constituency boundaries is usually given to an all-party committee, or to an (presumably) impartial judicial panel.

SIZE OF LEGISLATURE AND AVERAGE CONSTITUENCY (LOWER CHAMBER IN BICAMERAL LEGISLATURES, JULY 1999)			
COUNTRY	SEATS	POPULATION (MILLIONS)	CONSTITUENCY SIZE (POP / SEATS)
Finland	200	5.2	26,000
Hungary	386	10.2	26,000
Sweden	349	8.9	26,000
Norway	165	4.4	27,000
Denmark	179	5.4	30,000
New Zealand	120	3.7	31,000
Greece	300	10.7	36,000
Portugal	230	9.9	43,000
Austria	183	8.1	44,000
Israel	120	5.7	48,000
Czech Rep.	200	10.3	51,000
Ireland	60	3.6	61,000
Belgium	150	10.2	68,000
Poland	460	38.6	84,000
Italy	630	56.7	90,000
U.K.	659	59.1	90,000
France	577	59.0	102,000
Canada	301	31.0	103,000
Netherlands	150	15.8	105,000
Spain	350	39.2	112,000
Germany	669	82.1	123,000
Australia	148	18.8	127,000
Japan	500	126.2	252,000
Russia	450	146.4	325,000
U.S.	435	272.6	627,000
India	545	1,000.8	1,836,000

FIGURE 4.1

The point behind electoral boundary commissions and the broader principle of representation by population is that of fairness. Several other features of democratic systems are designed to provide fairness to the parties contesting the election. One is rules about the **FINANCING** of **ELECTION CAMPAIGNS**, rules which for the most part today are designed (not to say that they succeed) to minimize the influence of wealthy private or corporate donors and encourage broad public financing of political parties. Here the reasoning is that parties that are heavily reliant on support from narrow or particular interests cannot be expected to be fully responsive to the wishes of the broader public. So, too, no individual or group should be able to "buy an election." Congress has long wrestled with the question of money and influence in American elections, and there remain significant loopholes in the regulatory structure, particularly concerning the role of donations to national party organizations or "soft money." With a vocal minority arguing that any restriction on campaign money constitutes a violation of the constitutionally-guaranteed freedom of speech, the debate over campaign finance reform is unlikely to go away anytime soon (compare the position of the public interest group "Public Campaign," www.publicampaign.org/, for example, with that of Smith, 2001). In some European countries, there are severe restrictions on corporate or private contributions to political parties, but the latter receive monies from the public treasury, usually in proportion to the share vote received in the most recent election. On the other hand, in most European countries, laws requiring political parties to disclose private sources of funding are either weak or non-existent (Gallagher et al., 1995: 260).

Just as there are rules about financing, so, too, there are often restrictions concerning the use of the mass media and polling firms. In most European countries, (excepting Germany, Italy, and Sweden) political parties cannot purchase advertising time on television, although in many cases they receive an allocation of free time for political broadcasts. In Canada, political parties can purchase advertising time, but are limited to the share allocated each registered party from six and half hours of prime time in the last 39 days of the campaign. The allocation is determined largely (but not exclusively) on the basis of the party support received in the previous election and the number of seats held in the House of Commons. Parties also receive an amount of free time allocated in the same proportions. In the United States, however, there are no restrictions on the use of television. Another possible restriction altogether is the regulation of public opinion **POLLING**, usually in the very final stages of an election campaign. Once again, there are no restrictions on the release of poll data during American election campaigns. In Canada, regulations that prohibited the publication of a poll or commissioned survey in the last three days of the campaign were ruled unconstitutional by the Supreme Court. The New *Canada Elections Act*, passed in May 2000, prohibits the results of new election surveys during polling day. Such restrictions on the publication of polls are similar to restrictions evident in other democracies, where the period covered by the "gag-law" may be as long as a week.

Last but not least, we should consider the extent of the democratic **FRANCHISE** or the right to vote. Usually, but not always, the same rules determine who may or may not stand for election to office. Today, the franchise in the countries we have characterized as democratic is described as **UNIVERSAL ADULT SUFFRAGE**, meaning that—with a few exceptions such as those in prison, or deemed to be mentally incapacitated—all citizens above a certain age (usually 18 to 20) have the right to participate in elections as voters or candidates. The universality of voting rights today obscures how recently, in many cases, this universality has obtained. Women did not receive the vote until just after World War I in many cases and only following World War II in such countries as France and Italy, and 1971 in Switzerland (see Figure 4.2). New Zealand deserves credit for having extended the vote to women at a time when some countries still restricted the male vote to those holding sufficient property. At many different times the franchise has been withheld from people on the basis of their race, their religion, or their ethnic origin. That voting is usually restricted to citizens and that citizenship is seen to be incomplete without the right to vote indicate the symbolic importance of elections, something that may be as significant as anything we can say about their representative characteristics.

YEAR WOMEN GAINED VOTE

New Zealand	1893
Australia	1902
Canada	1918
Germany	1919
Sweden	1919
United States	1920
Britain	1928
Spain	1931
France	1944
Italy	1945
Japan	1945
Switzerland	1971

FIGURE 4.2

4.5 Electoral Systems: Main Variants

An **ELECTORAL SYSTEM** is a mechanism for transforming the preferences of citizens (votes) into an allocation of the offices at stake (seats in the legislature, a presidency) among the competing candidates—a sorting out of the winners and losers. In some ways an electoral system is a very simple institution, not much more than some rules and mathematical formulas (although the latter may test the arithmetically challenged). On the other hand, the consequences of electoral systems are considerable: for the party system, for the nature of representation that citizens receive, and for the nature of parliamentary government (discussed at greater length in Chapter 2). Because these consequences are most clearly attached to the selection of representatives for the legislature, this will be our focus: the electoral system as a means of translating votes (v) for competing candidates and parties into seats (s).

As in Chapter 2, we will make a distinction between those systems that tend (or are designed) to produce a majority outcome, hence **MAJORITARIAN ELECTORAL SYSTEMS**, and those systems that are designed to distribute seats proportionately among parties, hence **PROPORTIONATE ELECTORAL SYSTEMS**. Behind these distinctions (which are based on outcomes) are two variables that describe the basic features of an electoral system. One is the number of candidates elected in each of the constituencies (electoral districts), what is sometimes known as **DISTRICT MAGNITUDE** (*D*). The universe of electoral systems can be divided into those that have a *D* of 1, known as **SINGLE-MEMBER** systems, and those where *D* > 1, **MULTI-MEMBER** systems. Canada, the United States, and Britain each have single-member systems, where citizens choose one candidate per electoral district; it may surprise students from these countries to learn that in most of the world's democracies, citizens either choose two or more candidates in each electoral district, or cast separate votes for candidates and parties (a distinction explained below). The second variable is the **ELECTORAL FORMULA**, which is simply the rule by which the winner is (or winners are) determined. Three types of electoral formula are used: *plurality*, which indicates that the candidate (or candidates) with more votes than any other(s) is declared the winner; *majority*, which requires a winning candidate to secure a majority of the votes cast; and *proportionate*, which distributes seats among parties in roughly the proportion that the votes were cast. As may seem obvious, the plurality and majority formulas are associated usually with single-member systems, and the proportionate formula with multi-member systems. An overview of these variations is presented in Figure 4.3.

In comparing electoral system effects, again two broad variables can be noted. One is the amount of **DISPROPORTIONALITY**. In a perfectly proportionate system, the proportion of seats each party receives in the legislature is identical to the proportion of votes it received from the electorate; thus % s = % v. This is not simply a mathematical equation, but represents what some would argue is the ideal of **ELECTORAL JUSTICE**; where there is strict proportionality, the legislature reflects most accurately citizens' preferences; no party wins more or less seats than its share of the votes entitles it to. In this way, strict proportionality is extremely democratic. It is also something rarely achieved, although most proportionate systems come pretty close, and some very close indeed.

The second outcome variable is something called the **EFFECTIVE THRESHOLD**. This will determine how much support a party needs in order to gain seats in the legislature, and as a result,

ELECTORAL FORMULAS, DISTRICT MAGNITUDE, AND RESULTING SYSTEM

ELECTORAL FORMULA	DISTRICT MAGNITUDE	
	SINGLE-MEMBER	MULTI-MEMBER
PLURALITY	MAJORITARIAN (Britain, Canada, New Zealand [pre-1996], United States)	MAJORITARIAN (Japan [pre-1996]: this system had multi-member constituencies in which citizens cast one vote)
MAJORITY	MAJORITARIAN (France, Australia)	None
PROPORTIONATE	PROPORTIONATE (Germany, Italy, Japan [1996], New Zealand [1996]: although there are single-member districts, a second vote cast for party is used to ensure proportionality)	PROPORTIONATE (Austria, Belgium, Denmark, Greece, Iceland, Ireland, Luxembourg, Malta, Netherlands, Norway, Portugal, Spain, Sweden, Switzerland, and most East European democracies)

FIGURE 4.3

influence the number of parties in the legislature. In some proportionate systems there is a **LEGAL THRESHOLD**, a level of support that a party must receive in order to be allocated its share of legislature seats. In Germany, Italy, and New Zealand, for example, the threshold is (with exceptions) 5 per cent. Where there is no legal requirement, the features of the electoral system itself will determine the effective threshold. In the Netherlands, for example, there is one national constituency of 150 seats; this means that any party that can win more than 0.67 per cent of the vote will be guaranteed a seat in the legislature—this is a very low effective threshold. In a single-member plurality system like Canada's, Lijphart calculates the effective threshold to be 35 per cent (1994: 17). This doesn't mean a party must win 35 per cent of the vote to win seats, but that this level of support is required for a party to be reasonably assured of receiving a proportion of seats matching or exceeding its level of support. What matters here is that a high effective threshold will discourage or penalize new or small parties; a low threshold will have the opposite effect, all else being equal. Now let us consider the major types of systems a little more closely.

EXAMPLE ONE

	DISTRICT 1	DISTRICT 2	DISTRICT 3	DISTRICT 4	DISTRICT 5	TOTAL
Party A	1,500 v	1,200 v	800 v	750 v	668 v	4,918v
Party B	400 v	750 v	750 v	700 v	666 v	3,266v
Party C	100 v	50 v	450 v	550 v	666 v	1,816v

TOTAL	%V	%S
Party A	49.18	100
Party B	32.66	0
Party C	18.16	0

FIGURE 4.4

4.5.1 SINGLE-MEMBER (MAJORITARIAN) SYSTEMS

First and simplest are systems that elect a single member for each district, either by majority or plurality electoral formulae. Of these, the simplest is the **SINGLE-MEMBER PLURALITY (SMP)** system, which is common to the United States, the United Kingdom, and various other formerly British territories. The simplicity of the system is often presented as one of its virtues: citizens can understand it easily. In each constituency, eligible voters select one from a list of competing candidates and the candidate receiving more votes than any other is the winner. If there are only two candidates, as was once often (and in some cases—particularly in the U.S.—may still be) the case, the winner also will have a majority of votes. But as the number of candidates rises, the level of support with which it is possible to win decreases (for three candidates it is 33 per cent +1 vote, for four candidates it is 25 per cent +1 vote, for five candidates it is 20 per cent +1 vote, etc.), and it becomes more likely that the winner will have received less than a majority of votes cast in the electoral district (hence, the designation as a *plurality* system). This system is quite accurately described as a "winner take all" system; being a single-member constituency, there is just one prize, which the winner receives no matter how large or small the margin of victory. The other candidates, no matter how close they were to the winning level of support, win nothing at all. This feature affects the outcome of SMP systems in several ways.

First of all, it contributes to the likelihood of **DISPROPORTION-ALITY** (%s α %v); there is no necessary correspondence between the proportion of votes gained by each party, and its share of legislative seats. This is because *in each electoral district* one party wins 100 per cent of the seats with something less than 100 per cent of the vote.

EXAMPLE TWO

	DISTRICT 1	DISTRICT 2	DISTRICT 3	DISTRICT 4	DISTRICT 5	TOTAL
Party A	**700 V**	100 v	**820 V**	**730 V**	**880 V**	3,230v
Party B	690 v	800 v	600 v	630 v	720 v	3,440v
Party C	610 v	**1,100 V**	580 v	640 v	400 v	3,330v

TOTAL	%V	%S
Party A	32.3	80
Party B	34.4	0
Party C	33.3	20

FIGURE 4.5

When these results are added up nationally there is considerable chance of distortion, and no reason that these will somehow "balance out" among the parties. Figure 4.4 presents an extreme, but by no means impossible example for a very small parliament of five electoral districts. As this hypothetical example shows, even though Party *A* wins every district seat by finishing ahead of its rivals, overall its share of the votes cast is actually less than 50 per cent. In such a situation, a majority of citizens voting expressed a preference for legislators from parties *other* than *A*, but receive no representation in the legislature. Figure 4.5 presents an hypothetical result for our five seat parliament in which the party with the least support wins every seat but one, and the party with the most support is completely shut out.

The disproportionalities or distortions in outcome created by SMP systems are not random, but follow regular patterns. Because of the winner-take-all feature of the system, the party that has the largest share of vote tends (the previous example notwithstanding) to be "overpaid" by the system, receiving a larger share of seats than its share of vote would warrant. Correspondingly, when one party is overpaid, another (or more) must be penalized: in a two-party system this will be the second-place party, but where there are several parties it may be some or all of these in varying degrees. This tendency to overcompensate the winning party at the expense of others is the feature that allows SMP systems to generate single-party majority governments, but these majorities are generally inflated, and are often manufactured (like the example in Figure 4.5). For example, Canada has had 11 majority governments since 1945; of these only two had earned the support of more than 50 per cent of the electorate. Nine of 11 majority governments were **MANUFACTURED**, meaning that a majority of the electorate had actually voted against the government. A majority government based on minority support is in some respects a "false victory" produced by SMP. More rare are occasions when the party finishing second in voter support has received more seats in the legislature; this situation has occurred twice in Canadian history (1896, 1979). SMP is not necessarily responsive to changes in public opinion—parties can lose a little support and all their seats, or lose much support but few seats—and in some cases delivers a contrary result. At the very least, these kinds of results indicate that there is no necessary correspondence in this electoral system between inputs and outputs. If elections are to be a primary means for citizens to keep elites accountable, it seems curious to employ a system that fails to reflect accurately the public's expressed preferences.

The winner-take-all character of SMP is especially tough on new or small parties, and for this reason supports or sustains two-party systems in most cases (the United States is an example confirming this generalization, while Canada is a notable exception). A new party can succeed only in electoral districts where it becomes *the* most popular party; by the same token a party that finishes second in every electoral district has no more to show for its effort than a party that finishes tenth in every electoral district. New or small parties with evenly distributed, weak to moderate support will win little or nothing while new or small parties with regionally concentrated support can succeed, or even flourish, for a time. In this way SMP encourages regionalism or sectionalism, not only within the party system, but within parties themselves, which may seek to concentrate on areas where they already have support rather than seeking to strengthen their appeal in more marginal areas. Finally, SMP encourages strategic voting. This occurs when voters, anticipating a certain outcome, vote for a party other than their first choice in an attempt to prevent that outcome. It may be difficult to find a reason to vote for a party that has no realistic chance (given available evidence) of winning the seat. In this way votes cast for any candidate other than the one who wins are "wasted" votes—they count for nothing in the outcome.

In France and Australia, different electoral formulas have been combined with single member districts to produce results that are majoritarian, but here in either case, a simple plurality of votes will not suffice to win the constituency. These are sometimes called **SINGLE MEMBER MAJORITY** systems, but this is only partially (and not necessarily) true of the French legislative elections.

The distinctive feature of the French system is a second round of voting (or what is sometimes called a **RUN-OFF**) in constituencies where no candidate secures a majority of the votes cast in the

LEGISLATIVE ELECTION: FRANCE, 2002			
	% VALID BALLOTS		
PARTY	**1ST ROUND**	**2ND ROUND**	**SEATS # (%)**
Communist	4.9	3.3	21 (0.4%)
Socialist	23.8	35.3	140 (24.3%)
Other Left	5.6	3.5	13 (0.2%)
UDF	4.8	3.9	29 (5%)
UMP	33.4	47.3	355 (61.5%)
Other Right	6.5	1.6	12 (0.2%)
National Front	11.2	1.9	0 (0%)
Greens	4.4	3.2	3 (0.1%)
Other	5.4		3 (0.1%)

FIGURE 4.6

initial round. The second vote occurs a week following the first one. All candidates receiving less than 12.5 per cent of the vote in the first round are removed from the ballot for the second round. Whoever receives a plurality in the second round is the winner. In practice, this system encourages electoral co-operation between parties of the left and between parties of the right, parties within each group usually agreeing on whose candidate to support in the second round. This often has the result of reducing the number of effective candidates in the second round to two, which ensures that the winner has a majority of the votes cast. Nonetheless, this majority has also been manufactured: many will be forced to vote in the second for a party that represents their second or third choice, or not to vote at all. Similarly, there is no necessary correspondence between voter preferences and final party standings in the legislature. Figure 4.6 demonstrates some of these features of the French system in the context of the most recent legislative elections held in June 2002. The effect of the run-off is clearly to draw support from the minor parties and concentrate it with the large parties within each ideological division (note the increases across the two ballots in the popular vote for the Socialists and the Union for a Presidential Majority, or UMP). In terms of the final distribution of seats, the disproportionalities are considerable. The UMP, for example, was able to form a majority government with over 60 per cent of the seats in the National Assembly based on less than half the popular vote.

The Australian single-member system employs what is called an alternative vote, by means of an **ORDINAL** or **PREFERENTIAL BALLOT**. This means that instead of choosing one among the avail-

EFFECTS OF ELECTORAL FORMULAS ON DISPROPORTIONALITY AND PARTY SYSTEMS

ELECTORAL FORMULA	DISPROPOR-TIONALITY	EFFECTIVE NUMBER OF ELECTIVE PARTIES	EFFECTIVE NUMBER OF PARLIAMENTARY PARTIES	FREQUENCY OF PARLIAMENTARY MAJORITIES	FREQUENCY OF MANUFACTURED MAJORITIES
Plurality (5)	13.56	3.09	2.04	0.93	0.71
Other Majoritarian (2)	10.88	3.58	2.77	0.52	0.52
Proportionate (20)	4.27	4.07	3.56	0.20	0.12

Note: The number in brackets indicates the number of countries on which the numbers for each formula are based. Source: Adapted from Lijphart (1994: 96).

FIGURE 4.7

able candidates, voters rank all the candidates in order of preference. If no candidate should secure a majority of first preference votes, then the candidate with the least number of first preference votes is eliminated, and her/his ballots redistributed among the remaining candidates on the basis of the second preferences indicated. This process continues until one candidate has a majority of accumulated preferences. This can be a cumbersome and time-consuming process, particularly when there are large numbers of candidates.

One is tempted to call the French and Australian systems idiosyncratic variations on the majoritarian theme, measuring marginally better than simple plurality systems with respect to disproportionality and effective threshold (see Figure 4.7); as the table shows, they are also less likely to manufacture a parliamentary majority. The point is, however, that majoritarian systems, whether resting on plurality rules or not, are increasingly idiosyncratic in the democratic world, where the virtues of proportionality seem increasingly to rule.

4.5.2 PROPORTIONATE ELECTORAL SYSTEMS

The operation of plurality systems is easy to understand but the results can be puzzling; the outcome of proportionate systems, by contrast, is fairly transparent, but the various means employed to achieve this result can be complicated and confusing. The entire rationale of proportionate representation systems is to distribute

ELECTIONS IN THE 1990S

A: PLURALITY SYSTEMS

CANADA 2000	% V	# S	% S
Liberal	40.8	172	57.1
Canadian Alliance	25.5	66	21.9
Progressive Conservative	12.2	12	4.0
Bloc Québécois	10.7	38	12.6
New Democratic Party	8.5	13	4.3
Total		301	

BRITAIN 1997	% V	# S	% S
Labour	43.2	418	64.4
Conservative	30.7	165	25.0
Liberal Democrats	16.8	46	7.0
Referendum	2.6	—	—
Scottish National	2.0	6	0.9
Ulster Unionist	0.8	10	1.5
Social Democratic and Labour	0.6	3	0.5
Playd Cymru/Party of Wales	0.5	4	0.6
Sinn Fein	0.4	2	0.3
Democratic Unionist	0.3	2	0.3
Other	2.0	3	0.5
Total		659	

B: PROPORTIONATE SYSTEMS

BELGIUM 1999	% V	# S	% S
Flemish Liberals and Democrats	14.3	23	15.3
Christian People's (Flemish)	14.1	22	14.7
Socialists (Francophone)	10.1	19	12.7
Liberal Reformist	10.1	18	12.0
Flemish Bloc	9.9	15	10.0
Socialists (Flemish)	9.6	14	9.3
Francophone Ecologists	7.3	11	7.3
Flemish Ecologists	7.0	9	6.0
Christian Social (Francophone)	5.9	10	6.7
People's Union-ID21	5.6	8	5.3
National Front	1.5	1	0.7
Other	2.1	—	—
Total		150	

CZECH REPUBLIC 1998	% V	# S	% S
Social Democrats	32.3	74	37.0
Civic Democratic Party	27.7	63	31.5
Communists	11.0	24	12.0
Christian Democrats	9.0	20	10.0
Freedom Union	8.6	19	9.5
Rally for the Republic	3.9	—	—
Pensioners' Party	3.1	—	—
Democratic Union	1.4	—	—
Total		200	

DENMARK 1998	% V	# S	% S
Social Democrats	36.0	63	35.2
Liberals	24.0	42	23.5
Conservative People's Party	8.9	16	8.9
Socialists	7.5	13	7.3
Danish People's Party	7.4	13	7.3
Centre Democrats	4.3	8	4.5
Radical Left-Social Liberal	3.9	7	3.9
Unity List-The Red Greens	2.7	5	2.8
Christian People's Party	2.4	4	2.2
Progress Party	2.4	4	2.2
Others		4	2.2
Total		179	

FINLAND 1999	% V	# S	% S
Social Democrats	22.9	51	25.5
Centre Party	22.4	48	24.0
National Coalition Party	21.0	46	23.0
Left-Wing Alliance	10.9	20	10.0
Swedish People's Party	5.1	11	5.5
Greens	7.3	11	5.5
Finnish Christian League	4.2	10	5.0
Others	1.2	3	1.5
Total		200	

GERMANY 1998	% V	# S	% S
Social Democrats	40.9	298	44.5
C.D.U. / C.S.U.	35.1	245	36.6
Alliance 90-The Greens	6.7	47	7.0
Free Democrats	6.2	43	6.4
Party of Democratic Socialism	5.1	36	5.4
The Republicans	1.8	—	—
German People's Party	1.2	—	—
Total		669	

FIGURE 4.8

GREECE 2000	% V	# S	% S
Socialists	43.8	158	52.7
New Democracy	42.7	125	41.7
Communists	5.5	11	3.7
Left Coalition	3.2	6	2.0
Democratic Movement	2.7	—	—
Total		300	

NORWAY 1997	% V	# S	% S
Labour	35.1	65	39.4
Progress	15.3	25	15.2
Christian People's Party	13.7	25	15.2
Conservatives	14.3	23	13.9
Centre	8.0	11	6.7
Socialist Left	5.9	9	5.5
Liberal	4.5	6	3.6
Others	3.3	1	0.6
Total		165	

NETHERLANDS 1998	% V	# S	% S
Labour Party	29.0	45	30.0
People's Party	24.7	38	25.3
Christian Democratic Appeal	18.4	29	19.3
Democrats '66	9.0	14	9.3
Green Left	7.3	11	7.3
Socialists	3.5	5	3.3
Reformation Political Federation	2.0	3	2.0
Reformed Political League	1.3	2	1.3
Political Reformed Party	1.8	3	2.0
Total		150	

SWITZERLAND 1999	% V	# S	% S
Swiss People's Party	22.6	44	22.0
Social Democrats	22.5	51	25.5
Free Democrats	19.9	43	21.5
Christian Democratic People's Party	15.8	35	17.5
Green Party	5.0	9	4.5
Liberal Party	2.3	6	3.0
Swiss Democrats	1.8	1	0.5
Evangelical People's Party	1.8	3	1.5
Federal Democratic Union	1.3	1	0.5
Swiss Labour Party	1.0	2	1.0
League of Ticenesians	0.9	2	1.0
Freedom Party	0.9	1	0.5
Alliance of Independents	0.7	1	0.5
Sol	0.5	1	0.5
Christian Social Party	0.4	1	0.5
Total		200	

POLAND 1997	% V	# S	% S
Solidarity Electoral Action	33.8	201	43.7
Alliance of Democratic Left	27.1	164	35.7
Freedom Union	13.4	60	13.0
Polish People's Party	7.3	27	5.9
Reconstruction Movement	5.6	6	1.3
Union of Labour	4.4	—	—
Silesian Germans	.	2	0.4
Others	6.5	—	—
Total		460	

RUSSIA 1999	% V	# S	% S
Communists	24.3	113	25.1
Unity	23.2	72	16.0
Fatherland-All Russia	12.1	66	14.7
Union of Right Wing Forces	8.6	29	6.4
Zhirinovsky Bloc	6.0	17	3.7
Yabloko	6.0	21	4.7
Others and Independents	18.4	132	29.3
Total		450	

SPAIN 2000	% V	# S	% S
People's Party	44.6	183	52.3
Socialists	34.1	125	35.7
United Left	5.5	8	2.3
Convergence and Union of Catalonia	4.2	15	4.3
Basque Nationalist	1.5	7	2.0
Galician Nationalist Bloc	1.3	3	0.9
Canarian Coalition	1.1	4	1.1
Andalusian	0.9	1	0.3
Republican Left of Catalonia	0.8	1	0.3
Catalonian Greens	0.5	1	0.3
Basque Solidarity	0.4	1	0.3
Aragonese Junta	0.3	1	0.3
Total		350	

SWEDEN 1998	% V	# S	% S
Social Democrats	36.4	131	37.5
Moderates	22.9	82	23.5
Left-wing Party	12.0	43	12.3
Christian Democrats	11.8	42	12.0
Centre Party	5.1	18	5.2
People's Party Liberals	4.7	17	4.9
Greens	4.5	16	4.6
Total		349	

legislative seats among parties in proportions as true to their share of votes as is possible. This can be seen in the contrast, presented in Figure 4.8, between the distribution of seats and votes in plurality systems and in proportionate systems. There are three sets of distinctions we need to examine in order to understand how proportionate systems actually work. First of all, we have noted that proportionate systems often employ a multi-member constituency. The size of these constituencies can vary considerably, from three or four members up to a national constituency that effectively presents the whole legislature to each citizen (as in Israel and the Netherlands), but the normal range seems to be between five and 15 members returned to the legislature from each constituency. The larger the constituency the more easily a proportionate distribution of seats in the constituency will be. Consider an outcome like that noted above:

Party *A*	40%	Party *C*	20%
Party *B*	30%	Party *D*	10%

If there are four seats at stake here, the division (depending on the formula used) will be one seat for each party, or two for party *A* and one each for *B* and *C*. Neither division is very close to the actual proportions of support; with 10 seats at stake, each party could receive exactly the proportion of seats warranted by its vote share: four for *A*, three for *B*, two for *C*, and one for *D*. The trade-off for greater proportionality is a more distant relationship between representatives on the one hand and citizens and localities on the other as constituencies become larger and more populous.

Given the number of parties that may be contesting the election, multi-member constituencies obviously involve a different balloting environment than that of single-member plurality systems. In two countries, Ireland and Malta, the voters employ a **SINGLE TRANSFERABLE VOTE** (**STV**), which is (like the Australian ballot) an ordinal ballot in which voters rank the candidates in order of preference. Unlike the Australian case, here several candidates will be elected, so the ballot may be quite lengthy, and counting procedures quite complicated. One virtue of STV is that it gives the voters a maximum freedom to choose among candidates of different parties and express their preferences for them.

Much more common in multi-member constituencies are **LIST SYSTEMS**, where voters choose between party lists. In a six-member constituency, each party contesting the election will present voters with a list of candidates for consideration (see Figure

4.9). List systems vary considerably with regard to the amount of choice they present to voters. In some cases, voters will have simply the choice of one party's list, or another's. In other cases they are able to change the order of candidates, who appear on the ballot in an order determined by the party. Control over the ranking of candidates clearly is crucial to their electability (and it is also a very effective means of exercising party discipline). Obviously, in a six-member electoral district, given proportionality, it is extremely unlikely that a party will elect all of its candidates. Those at the top of the list will be the first elected; in the sample ballot shown, the party has attempted to increase the chances of electing its first candidate. Casting this ballot would give six votes to the Radical Party, two to Brigitte Barker, and one to each of the other candidates. The maximum amount of flexibility is perhaps exhibited in the degree of choice that the Swiss system gives to voters. They may scratch names off a party ballot, and write in names of individuals from other parties, thus indicating that while they wish to support a particular party, they also want to influence the determination of which representatives are elected from the other parties. In addition, the Swiss are given a blank ballot, on which the voter may write the names of candidates from any of the party ballots supplied to them. As in so many other areas, though, Swiss practice here is exceptional rather than typical.

Perhaps the most complicated aspect of proportionate systems, and one that really is exciting only to the specialist or the mathematically inclined, is the actual formula by which seats are allocated within the constituency. Various rules are applied to determine the allocation of seats within specific PR systems, and these differ in their overall tendency to favor small or large parties, but compared with the disproportionalities of SMP, these variations normally are small. Two types of formula are used: highest averages (the D'Hondt and modified Sainte-Laguë systems) and largest remainders (the Hare, Droop, and Imperiali quotas being those in use). The application of these systems is rather complicated and not something we need to explore further here, but Figure 4.10 illustrates the different allocation of seats that each method would make for the same results in an eight-member constituency with 100,000 votes cast.

The results in Figure 4.10 show that there is a slight difference within each type of formula in the outcomes generated. In the case shown, the D'Hondt system and Droop and Imperiali quotas favor the largest party, and the Sainte-Laguë method and

RADICAL
ballot October 21, 1999
PARTY: Radical
LIST: #02

ELECTION OF SIX MEMBERS OF PARLIAMENT
02.01 Barker, Brigitte
      Barker, Brigitte
02.02 Dali, Georg
02.03 Feingold, Isaac
02.04 Lewis, Cynthia
02.05 Zubac, Jan

FIGURE 4.9

PROPORTIONAL ELECTORAL FORMULAS

PARTY	VOTES	HIGHEST AVERAGES		LARGEST REMAINDERS		
		D'HONDT	SAINTE-LAGUË	HARE	DROOP	IMPERIALI
Party A	32,000	3	2	2	3	3
Party B	24,000	2	2	2	2	2
Party C	20,000	1	2	2	1	1
Party D	13,500	1	1	1	1	1
Party E	10,500	1	1	1	1	1

FIGURE 4.10

Hare quota favor the smaller parties, although here it is the middle party that benefits.

As may be obvious, while these methods obviously award seats in a much more proportional way than a plurality or majoritarian formula, strict proportionality is still not achieved on a constituency basis unless the constituency (or district magnitude = D) is very large. As Figure 4.8 demonstrates, results in the Netherlands, which has one national constituency, are extremely proportional. Since most systems employ smaller constituencies, they often also use what is called a **SECOND TIER**. This means that not all seats are allocated through the balloting for candidates in the constituencies; some are held back for a second round of allocation, the purpose of which—generally—is to adjust for any disproportionalities created by the constituency allocation of seats (i.e., the first round). Countries that employ a two-tier system include Austria, Belgium, Denmark, Germany, Greece, Iceland, Italy, Malta, Norway, and Sweden. For the second tier, district magnitude is usually much larger than for the first tier, and often is a national constituency. The electoral formula is also usually different from that employed at the first tier. Depending on thresholds, legal or effective, the second tier may exclude smaller parties, or in fact ensure that they receive seats. The amount of disproportionality generated by the Greek system (see Figure 4.8) has a lot to do with the high threshold for participation in second-tier allocation of seats; this means the larger parties are rewarded. If, as is usually the case, the purpose of the second-tier seats is to eliminate disproportionalities created in the first-tier allocation, then the number of second-tier seats necessary will be determined by the level of disproportionality that the first tier generates. (The second-tier seats, for this reason, are often called **ADJUSTMENT SEATS**.) If the total discrepancy between share of votes and seats that parties ought to receive is small, then the second tier can be small, also. As a general rule, the smaller the first-tier constituencies, the larger the possibility of disproportionality, and hence the larger the second tier will need to be.

4.5.3 HYBRID (MIXED-MEMBER) SYSTEMS

This brings us to what seems to be emerging as one of the more popular forms of PR, a two-tier system that combines the virtue of single-member districts (e.g., attachment of a representative to a local constituency) with the justice of proportional outcomes. The model here is the German system, in which half (50 per cent) of the seats for the Bundestag are elected by voters choosing a candidate in single-member constituencies. Victory in the local constituency requires simply a plurality of votes cast. At the same time, though, German voters also cast a vote for the party of their choice, a vote which is quite separate from their vote for a local representative in parliament, and which allows them to choose who they think is the best candidate without compromising their support for a national party. The "party vote" is used to determine the ultimate allocation of seats in the legislature. The seats not allocated through the single-member districts (i.e., the other 50 per cent) are used as adjustment seats in a national constituency and are allocated in such a way that the *total* seats in the Bundestag is proportionate to a party's support as registered by the party half of the ballot. The German system has a legal threshold; parties that do not receive at least 5 per cent of the party vote are ineligible for second-tier seats, unless they win at least three first-tier seats. In the latter case they are entitled to a share of the second-tier seats that will deliver a proportionate result, even if their party vote was below the threshold. One remaining puzzle, perhaps, is how the second- or upper-tier seats are actually allocated among party members. In the German case, each party ranks all its candidates, from party leader down. The upper-tier seats will go in order to those on the party list who failed to win a lower-tier seat. This is another case where party control over candidate-ranking may be a powerful tool of party discipline.

In two other countries, a switch to a "German-style" proportionate system has been made in the attempt to address problems in the party system and parliament. In 1996, New Zealand held its first election under a new proportional system with 65 single-member seats and 55 proportional or adjustment seats. This is obviously very much like the German system, and transforms one of the few remaining plurality system countries into the proportionate family.

Significantly, this reform of the electoral system was approved by the people of New Zealand in a national referendum. The intent was to inject fairness and responsiveness into a system that tended to favor the two largest parties, which in turn were seen by many to be too much alike. Also at the end of 1996, Japan inaugurated a new electoral system with 300 single-member seats and 200 proportional seats chosen in 11 regional constituencies. Here the intent was to reform a multi-member plurality system that had been dominated by the (often corrupt) LDP. Japan, incidentally, is the only industrial democracy that requires voters to write in full the names of the candidates of their choice.

4.6
Party Systems

Electoral systems matter because of the outputs they deliver, which are first and foremost a party system and, out of that party system, a pattern of government formation. We discussed patterns of government formation in Chapter 2. To conclude this chapter, we need to make some observations about party systems, where a party system is a "set of political parties operating within a nation [polity] in an organized pattern, described by a number of party-system properties" (Lane and Ersson, 1991: 175). This system, most observers agree, is something larger than the sum of its parts, and the behavior and characteristics of individual parties are shaped by the systems within which they operate and, more specifically, by the properties of those systems. We will look at just three system properties: the size of the system, its ideological polarization, and its capacity to express distinct issue dimensions.

We have noted the principal features of plurality systems: their tendency to manufacture majorities by over-rewarding winning parties; their overcompensation of regionally concentrated parties; and the penalization of parties with diffuse but moderate to weak strength. The winner-take-all character of such systems also puts a very large hurdle in the way of new parties; to win a seat, a new party must finish ahead of all the established parties in the electoral district. To gain 15, 20, or even 30 per cent of the vote is something of an accomplishment for a new party, particularly if it can do this in several or many electoral districts, and over the course of two or more elections. Nonetheless, this level of support is meaningless unless within specific electoral districts it means finishing first: there is no prize for finishing second, even if that has been 49.99 per cent of the votes cast. Not surprisingly, then, most plurality systems tend to sustain a two-party system.

Proportionate systems are almost uniformly associated with multi-party systems. The combination of several parties with more or less strict proportionality means that a one-party majority is unlikely, and is almost never manufactured (see Figure 4.8). It is normal, therefore, for the government in PR systems to be a coalition. Defenders of plurality systems are usually quick to associate coalition government with instability, and point to Italy's series of short-lived governments since 1945 to demonstrate the undesirable side-effects of a proportionate system. There is, though, little conclusive evidence that PR (or coalition government) produces instability, or, that the instability associated with rapidly changing governments has detrimental consequences. In many cases the new government contains many of the same partners as the old. Where governments are single-party majorities, by contrast, government change may well mean significantly new directions for public policy. For every Italy, there is a Switzerland *and* a Germany *and* a Luxembourg, where stability and coalition seem on intimate terms. What is beyond dispute is the responsiveness of proportionate systems to changes in public opinion; any increase or decline in a party's support is immediately and accurately reflected in its legislative standing, a feature bound to effect the way parties behave towards their supporters and others. If the existing parties are unsatisfactory to significant portions of the population, then new parties appealing to those sections of the electorate will form, and are more likely to succeed under a proportionate system than under single-member plurality, the only barrier being the legal threshold (which may, of course, be a significant barrier). Regional parties are also unlikely to have a monopoly of representation in their region, as is often the case under plurality rules.

We have been referring to two-party and multi-party systems without defining our terms adequately. In fact, determining the size of a party system is not the same as simply counting the number of parties. In the case of the U.S. Congress, or the first several Canadian general elections, where there were (and are) in fact only two parties, the judgment that we are talking about two-party systems is rather obvious. But what about the situation where a third party emerges and wins a few seats; how does this change the picture? To say that the picture is unchanged until the third party becomes sufficiently large enough just raises the further question: what is sufficiently large enough? These kinds of questions have prompted political scientists to generate an index that measures the **EFFECTIVE NUMBER OF PARTIES** based on a combination of their numbers *and* their relative strength. Thus, the British parliament (see Figure 4.8)

EFFECTIVE PARTIES (N)

The number (N) of effective parties is calculated for various numbers
of parties and distributions of support (either votes or seats).

2 PARTIES

A: 50%		A: 65%		A: 85%	
B: 50%	N = 2.0	B: 35%	N = 1.83	B: 15%	N = 1.34

3 PARTIES

A: 34%		A: 45%		A: 85%	
B: 33%		B: 45%		B: 10%	
C: 33%	N = 3.0	C:10%	N = 2.41	C: 5%	N = 1.36

4 PARTIES

A: 25%		A: 40%		A: 45%		A: 85%	
B: 25%		B: 30%		B: 40%		B: 5%	
C: 25%		C: 20%		C: 10%		C: 5%	
D: 25%	N = 4.0	D: 10%	N = 3.33	D: 5%	N = 2.67	D: 5%	N = 1.37

FIGURE 4.11

contains what is virtually a two-party system, even though seven parties have representation, because the two largest parties contain more than 88 per cent of the seats between them. Figure 4.12 shows how different distributions of support between parties affect the number of effective parties, and how distribution of support between parties rather than number of parties is the key variable.

In addition, we should note the difference between **ELECTIVE PARTIES** and **LEGISLATIVE PARTIES**. In virtually every election there is a difference between the number of parties that contest the election and the number of parties that actually win seats in the legislature. The former are elective parties, the latter are legislative parties. As Figure 4.8 and other data we have presented indicate, the electoral system has a large effect on the difference between the number of elective and legislative parties. Generally speaking, the electoral system presents more hurdles to elective parties in a plurality system than in a proportionate system (this is known as Duverger's "mechanical effect"). At the same time this effect is compounding: voters who know that minor parties will not receive their share of seats in plurality systems will consider votes for these parties "wasted" and vote strategically for other parties they may in fact prefer less (this is known as Duverger's "psychological effect"). Figure 4.12 shows the effective numbers of elective and legislative parties for a selection of elections in the 1990s. Depending on legal thresholds, proportionate systems will admit a larger portion of the elective parties into the legislature (thus Greece with its large threshold has a low number of legislative parties). In some cases, though, there is very little difference at all between the number of elective and legislative parties, and generally the proportionate systems produce multi-party systems.

Perhaps even more significant than the number of parties in the system (but much more difficult to measure) is the degree of choice it presents to the voters. It hardly matters if there are two or 12 parties if the policy choices that they present to the voters are pretty much indistinguishable. Conceptually, determining the degree of *polarization* entails plotting the position of parties on a right-left ideological scale and observing the patterns that result. Consider two very different situations within a two-party system:

ELECTIVE/LEGISLATIVE PARTIES [EFFECTIVE NUMBER (N)]			
COUNTRY	ELECTIVE	LEGIS-LATIVE	DIFFER-ENCE
Canada ('93)	3.93	2.35	−1.58
Britain ('92)	3.09	2.27	−0.82
Czech R. ('96)	5.40	4.15	−1.25
Denmark ('94)	4.75	4.73	−0.02
Germany ('94)	3.16	2.90	−0.26
Greece ('96)	3.08	2.36	−0.72
Netherlands ('94)	5.72	5.41	−0.31
Spain ('93)	3.54	2.68	−0.86
Sweden ('94)	3.64	3.48	−0.16

FIGURE 4.12

Clearly situation *A* is very unpolarized, while *B* presents an extremely polarized scenario. It is not unfair to suggest that American politics has often resembled *A*, and *B* has at various times been true of British party politics (particularly at the start of Mrs. Thatcher's tenure in office). Situation *B* offers a much clearer choice to voters than *A*, but a single-party government in *B* will be extremely distasteful to its non-supporters, while one could argue that it doesn't make much difference in *A* which party governs.

Similar patterns are common in multi-party systems, which, perhaps not surprisingly, can often be grouped into families—parties of the right, of the left, etc. Hence, we could substitute Germany for the U.S., noting that the two dominant right and left parties tend to converge on the center, and for Britain substitute Italy with parties ranged across the ideological spectrum, from the refounded Communists on the left to the neo-fascists on the right. Here, too, is a contrast between political competition played out at the center, and a contest covering a broader ideological range. It could be argued that all else being equal, a party system providing a range of ideological positions presents clearer choices to citizens and offers the conditions for a more meaningful political discourse about policy issues. Parties competing at the center are more likely to craft platforms that do not differ greatly in substance, shifting attention to issues of character and personality of candidates and leaders.

We should perhaps point out that not all competition is evenly balanced on either side of a "neutral" center. By definition, whichever party controls the median voter is at the center of the country's political culture. Hence, in Sweden, ranging the parties ideologically from left to right results in the following:

LEFT PARTY	SOCIAL DEMOCRATS	GREENS	CENTER	LIBERALS	CHRISTIAN DEMOCRATS	MODERATES
22	162	18	27	26	14	80

Interestingly, while the Center party is in one sense centrally located—three parties sit to its left, three to its right—the median vote in the legislature (the halfway point starting from right or left) is controlled by the Social Democrats, which means they are in the center. At the same time the strength of the Social Democrats and the distance between them and the second place Moderates at the far end of the spectrum suggests a fair degree of polarization in this party system. On a polarization index which generates an average for 16 European democracies of 3.1 in the period between 1945-89, Lane and Ersson (1991: 185) report a high of 5.1 for France and a low of 0.9 for Ireland.

It is also the case that the center is not fixed, but moves in one direction or another as the political culture changes. There are differences between countries (in both the U.S. and Germany, the major parties converge on the center, but the American center is much to the right of the German center), but also within countries over time. American parties have (almost) always competed at the center for the middle-class voter, but most observers would probably agree that this center has shifted considerably to the right in the last two decades—as indeed, it has in most industrial democracies. To what degree this is a temporary reaction to the accumulated deficits that governments have faced in this period, or a real shift in principle, remains to be seen.

Finally, we may note that the right-left classification of parties is itself suspect. On the one hand, the assessment of where a party falls on this scale is always a judgment call and not a matter of exact science. In addition, though, most right-left scales are largely concerned with party policy positions concerning socio-economic policy, issues that deal with what has been discussed as the class cleavage. As Lijphart (1994) argues, there are at least six other **ISSUE DIMENSIONS** that play a role in at least some of the stable democracies we have been considering: the religious, cultural-ethnic, urban-rural, regime support, foreign policy, and post-materialist issue dimensions. Parties that may be poles apart on questions of socio-economic policy may be close allies on the religious dimension, while a third set of allies links up on foreign policy questions. The presence of different issue dimensions poses intriguing challenges for government formation and explains many of the sources of internal division between coalition partners. Lijphart has calculated the number of relevant issue dimensions for 22 democracies in the 1945-80 period, ranging from a low of 1.0 in Ireland, New Zealand, and the United States; to a high of 3.5 in France, Norway, and Finland (1994: 130). Perhaps more striking is the fairly strong correlation he finds between the number of issue dimensions present and the number of effective parties. The higher the number of effective parties, the more issue dimensions a party system seems able to accommodate. This implies that multi-party systems will be better able to accommodate multiple issue dimensions (and thus, conceivably, accommodate social cleavages) than two-party (duopolistic) systems. This again, suggests an advantage to proportional systems compared with single-member plurality electoral machinery.

4.7 Conclusion

To summarize, electoral systems determine the distribution of legislative seats among the competing political parties in a great variety of manners. The electoral and legislative party systems created by the electoral system are significant outputs that are at the heart of democratic politics. The legislative party system will determine the government of the day, and distinct types of party systems lead to significantly different kinds of government, as discussed in Chapter 2. At the same time, the nature of the electoral party system and the degree to which popular preferences for political parties are reflected in the legislature will have a great influence on the organization and strategy of political parties, considered as actors in the drama of democracy.

It has no doubt also become obvious that the authors of this text have a clear preference for proportionate systems over the single-member plurality systems that have dominated the Anglo-

KEY TERMS

adjustment seats
ascriptive variables
class
constituency size
cross-cutting cleavages
disproportionality
district
district magnitude
effective number of parties
effective threshold
election financing

elective parties
electoral formula
electoral justice
electoral system
ethnicity
fragmentation
franchise
German-style PR
gerrymandering
hinterland
identities
interest
issue dimensions
linguistic cleavage
latent cleavage
legal threshold
legislative parties
list system
majoritarian system
manufactured majority
metropole
Mixed-Member System
multi-member constituency
ordinal ballot
parliamentary system
party system
periphery
plurality
polarization
political advertising
polling
population
preferential ballot
proportionality
representation by
population
race
regionalism
reinforcing cleavages
religion
"run-off"
second tier
secularism
separatism
single-member electoral
district
single-member majority
single-member plurality
single transferable vote
universal adult franchise
"winner take all"

American world. To put the argument most simply, the plurality system emerged in a time that was much simpler, in social, political, and technological terms, but has little to recommend it to today's complex, pluralistic societies. The principal virtue of plurality is its ability to return a majority government to Parliament, but the degree to which this is in fact a virtue needs critical examination, particularly considered against the costs of manufacturing such a majority through a system that is by no means consistently responsive to the preferences of voters.

REFERENCES AND FURTHER READING

Bennett, W. Lance. 1992. *The Governing Crisis*. New York: St. Martin's Press.

Bogdanor, Vernon, and David Butler. 1983. *Democracy and Elections*. Cambridge: Cambridge University Press.

Crewe, Ivor, and David Denver. 1985. *Electoral Change in Western Democracies*. London: Croom Helm.

Duverger, Maurice. 1963. *Political Parties*. New York: Wiley.

Gallagher, Michael, Michael Laver, and Peter Mair, eds. 1992. *Representative Government in Western Europe*. New York: McGraw-Hill.

Katz, Richard S. 1997. *Democracy and Elections*. Oxford: Oxford University Press.

Kelley, Stanley. 1983. *Interpreting Elections*. Princeton, NJ: Princeton University Press.

Lakeman, Enid. 1974. *How Democracies Vote*, 4th ed. London: Faber and Faber.

Lane, Jan-Erik, and Svante O. Ersson. 1991. *Politics and Society in Western Europe*. London: Sage Publications.

Lijphart, Arend. 1994. *Electoral Systems and Party Systems: A Study of Twenty-Seven Democracies, 1945-1990*. Oxford: Oxford University Press.

Patterson, Thomas C. 2002. *The Vanishing Voter: Public Involvement in an Age of Uncertainty*. New York: Alfred A. Knopf.

Penniman, Howard, and Austin Ranney, eds. 1981. *Democracy at the Polls: A Comparative Study of Competitive National Elections*. Washington: American Enterprise Institute.

Public Campaign. 2002. "Clean Money Campaign Reform." Available at: <http://www.publicampaign.org/publications/CleanMoneyCampaign Reform.pdf>.

Shugart, Matthew Soberg, and Martin P. Wattenberg, eds. 2001. *Mixed-Member Electoral Systems: The Best of Both Worlds?* Oxford: Oxford University Press.

Smith, Bradley A. 2001. *Unfree Speech: The Folly of Campaign Finance Reform*. Princeton, NJ: Princeton University Press.

INDEX

absolute monarchy. *See* monarchy
abstract review (judicial review), 26
access to information, 35
adjudication, 17–18
adjustment seats, 122
Administration (US), 39
amending formulas, 13, 15, 17, 28
American Bill of Rights. *See* Bill of Rights
American engagement in politics. *See* citizen participation
Andalusia, 91
aristocracy, 22, 29, 32
Aristotle, 29
ascriptive variables, 98
assassination, 56
asymmetrical federalism, 89
Australia, 25, 48, 60–61, 66, 77, 87
bicameral legislature, 19
as common law country, 14
constituency size, 108
constitution
  amending formula, 16–17
  paramountcy, 80
dual executive, 23
electoral formula, 112, 115–16
strong bicameralism, 86
women's vote, 110
Austria, 25, 41, 48, 61, 92, 105, 122
cabinet size, 62
constituency size, 108
constitutional court, 25
dual executive, 23
electoral formula, 112
authority, 14, 17
delegation, 76
depersonalization, 7
discretionary, 20
formal, 20

autonomy, 76, 78, 90–91. *See also* power

Bagehot, Walter, 11
Balladur, Edouard, 68
Basque Country, 91
Becker, Theodore, 24
Belarus, 60
Belgium, 25, 48, 50, 61, 77, 91, 105, 122
  cabinet size, 62
  constituency size, 108
  election (1999), 118
  electoral formula, 112
  ethno-linguistic cleavages, 101
  executive, 23
bicameral legislatures, 19–20, 42, 65, 85
  strong bicameralism, 42, 66, 86–87
Bill of Rights, 15, 30
Blair, Tony, 88–89
block grants, 84. *See also* transfer payments
Bosnia
  religious difference, 100
Brazil, 77
British North America Act of 1867, 17, 79
Bulgaria, 92
bureaucracy, 9, 20, 39, 64

cabinet, 22–23, 44, 49
  American cabinet secretaries, 39
  central institution of parliamentary system, 61
  as collective executive, 32, 45
  discretionary power, 31
  internal dissension, 57
  model of decision making, 64

  policy-making, 63
  size of, 62
  solidarity, 45, 64–65
  structure, 63
cabinet government, 35, 64
  origin of, 31–32
Canada, 48, 60–61, 83, 111
  bicameral legislature, 19
  British North America Act, 17, 79
  center-periphery cleavage, 102
  from centralized to decentralized federation, 80
  Charter of Rights and Freedoms, 15
  as common law country, 14
  constituency size, 108
  constitution, 13, 82
    amending procedure, 17
  election (2000), 118
  electoral system, 47, 112
  ethno-linguistic cleavages, 77, 101–2
  executive, 23
  "Fathers of Confederation," 79
  federal paramountcy, 80
  Governor-General, 21, 60–61, 88
  judicial review, 25
    reference, 25
  majority governments, 114
  party system, 115
  political advertising, 109
  provincial jurisdiction, 81
  publication of polls, 109–10
  as quasi-federal, 77
  Senate, 85–86, 88–89
  transfer payments, 84
  women's vote, 110
Canada Elections Act (2000), 109
caretaker governments, 55

termination, 59
Catalonia, 91
categorical grants, 84
caucus. *See* parliamentary party
censure, 67. *See also* confidence
center-periphery cleavages,
    101–2
centralization of power, 73–74
Charter of Rights and
    Freedoms, 15
checks and balances, 15, 28, 30,
    38, 41
Chirac, Jacques, 67–69
citizen participation, 27, 106
    distrust of government, 27
    educated citizenry, 35
    voter preferences, 116, 124,
        129–30
    voter turnout, 44
citizens' rights. *See* rights codes
class, 88, 101, 103–5
cleavages
    ascriptive variables, 98
    center-periphery, 101–2
    class, 103–5
    cross-cutting, 105
    definitions, 97–98
    ethno-linguistic, 101–2
    latent, 103–4
    perception of difference, 99
    reinforcing cleavages, 105
    religious difference, 100, 105
    urban-rural, 102–3
Clinton, Bill, 42
coalition government, 50–52,
    54, 125
    electoral coalition, 51
    executive coalition, 50–52, 57
    instability, 58
    legislative coalition, 51–52
    surplus majority, 57
    termination, 59
code of citizens' rights. *See*
    rights codes
cohabitation, 68–69
collective executive. *See* cabinet
Colombia, 71
common law, 13–14
communications infrastructures,
    11
"Concrete" review, 25
confederation, 75, 79
confidence, 32, 44, 55, 63
    chamber, 86
    constructive non-confi-
        dence, 56
    degrees, 56
    non-confidence, 87
Congress, 28–29
constituency, 107–8, 122
constitutional challenges, 25
constitutional courts, 12, 25
constitutional monarchy, 21
constitutionalism, 11
    ethic of, 13–14
    normative character, 12
constitutions, 8
    amendments and amending
        procedures, 13, 15–17,
        28, 81
    definition, 10
    entrenched documents, 14
    federal, 78
    formal, 14
    material, 11, 14, 68
    written, 11, 13–14
conventions, 14, 33, 53
    of responsible government,
        34
Costa Rica, 71
courts, 13, 24
    constitutional, 12, 25
    high or supreme, 12, 25,
        29–30, 81, 109
    political role, 24
cross-cutting cleavages, 105

cultural and ethnic distinctiveness. *See* ethno-linguistic cleavages
Cyprus, 92
religious difference, 100
Czech Republic, 92, 108
election (1998), 118

De Gaulle, Charles, 67
Debré, Michel, 67
decentralization, 77, 90
Canada, 82
Scandinavian countries, 91
decision-making, 8–9, 17
decolonization, 35
delegation of power or authority, 18, 76
democracy, 29, 35, 88
American-style, 37
pluralist, 37
waves of, 35
Denmark, 25, 48, 50, 61, 90, 92,
122
cabinet size, 62
constituency size, 108
election (1998), 118
electoral formula, 112
executive, 23
unicameral legislature, 19
depersonalization of power and
authority, 7
devolution, 89–90
D'Hondt system, 121–22
difference in interests, 99
discretionary authority, 20–23
disproportionality, 47, 111,
113–14, 116–17, 122
dissolution, 54. *See under* termination of governments
district magnitude, 111, 122
division of powers, 78, 85.
See also provincial
jurisdiction; separation

of powers
downsizing of government
activity, 82
Droop quota, 121–22
dual executive, 22–23, 45, 68
Duverger, Maurice
"mechanical effect," 126
"psychological effect," 126
dyarchy. *See* dual executive

economic redistribution, 11
effective number of parties,
125, 129
effective threshold, 111–12
"elastic clause," 79
elections, 54, 118
electoral schedule, 42
financing campaigns, 108–9
fixed electoral terms, 41–42,
55
free, 35, 70
mass media and polling, 109
popular control, 66
electoral coalition. *See* coalition
government
electoral districts, 108
electoral formulas, 111–12, 115
effect on disproportionality,
117
electoral justice, 111
electoral participation. *See*
citizen participation;
voter preference
electoral parties, 40
electoral systems, 46–47,
106–29
district magnitude, 111, 122
majoritarian, 111
mechanical effect, 126
plurality, 46, 49, 51, 108, 111
proportionate representation,
117–22
psychological effect, 127

single-member plurality (SMP), 113–16
emergency powers, 40
enforcement, 11
Enlightenment liberal view. *See* liberal revolution
entrenched documents, 14
Estonia, 92
ethno-linguistic cleavages, 77, 91, 101–2, 129
European Coal and Steel Community, 91
European Commission, 92–93
European Parliament, 92–93
European Union, 91–92
    Council of Ministers, 93–94
    Court of Justice, 92–93
executive coalition, 51–52, 57. *See under* coalition government
executive dominance, 35, 63–65
Executive Office of the President, 39
executives, 9, 17, 20–23
    cabinet, 23
    dual, 23
    formal, 21–22, 45
    mixed, 23
    political, 22, 38, 61, 71
    single, 23
    unified, 29

Faroe Islands, 90
federalism, 16, 81, 85
    asymmetrical, 89
    Canada, 17
    definition, 75–76
    division of powers, 78–89
    federal bargain, 78, 81–82
    quasi-federalism, 77
    safeguarding cultural entities, 77
    supranational federalism, 91

Finland, 25, 48, 50, 60–61, 69, 92
    cabinet size, 62
    constituency size, 108
    election (1999), 118
    election of president, 38
    executive, 23
    strong presidency, 66
fiscal powers, 11
    imbalance, 83
fiscal transfers. *See* transfer payments
foreign policy, 40, 129
formal executive, 21–22, 45
formateur, 53–54
fragmentation of powers. *See* separation of powers
France, 48, 50, 60–61, 69, 91
    bicameral legislature, 19
    constituency size, 108
    constitution, 37
    Constitutional Council, 25
    constitutional court, 25
    election of president, 38
    electoral formula, 112, 115–16
    executive, 23
    National Assembly, 67, 69
    women's vote, 110
France (Fifth Republic), 38, 62, 67–68
    hybrid system, 38, 123–24
    strong presidency, 66, 68
France (Fourth Republic), 58, 62, 67
franchise
    African Americans, 108
    universal franchise, 107
    women's vote, 107, 110
free elections, 35, 70
free press, 35
functions of the state, 7–11, 14, 17
fused powers, 23

fusion of powers, 32–33, 44–45

gag-laws, 110
Galicia, 91
George I, king, 33
Germany, 25, 48, 50, 55–56, 58, 61, 66, 83, 85, 87, 91, 109, 122
  Basic Law, 10, 13, 80, 82
    amending formula, 17
  bicameral legislature, 19
  cabinet size, 62
  constituency size, 108
  constitutional court, 25
  election (1998), 118
  electoral formula, 112
  executive, 23
  strong bicameralism, 86
  women's vote, 110
gerrymandering, 108
Glorious Revolution. See Whig Revolution of 1688
government. See also state
  dispersed powers of, 26
  downsizing, 82
  expansion of, 82
  formation, 52–53
  functions or purposes, 7–8
  head of, 125
  minimizing role of, 70
  municipal or local, 76
  offloading responsibilities, 82
  public dissatisfaction with, 44 (See also citizen participation)
  stability, 7, 54, 125
  weak, 41
Governor-General, 21, 60–61, 88
Governor-General (Australia) dismissed Labour government, 87
grand coalition, 57

grants-in-aid, 84. See also transfer payments
Great Britain. See United Kingdom
Greece, 61, 92, 108, 122, 127
  election (2000), 119
  electoral formula, 112
  executive, 23
  proportionate system, 48
Greenland, 90
growth of the state, 30, 62

Hare quota, 121–22
head of government, 23
head of state, 21, 45
  as above partisan politics, 61
  monarch, 60
  parliamentary system, 60–61
high courts. See Supreme Courts
Hill, Christopher, 33
hinterland, 102
home rule, 89–90
House of Commons (Canada), 86
House of Commons (UK), 32
House of Lords, 32
  suspensive veto, 88
House of Lords Bill, 88
House of Representatives, 29, 42
Hungary, 92, 108
hybrid systems, 38, 123–24

Iceland, 25, 48, 61, 122
  electoral formula, 112
  executive, 23
identity
  basis of, 104
  fragmentation of, 106
Imperiali quota, 121–22
implementation of policy, 17–18, 44

"incongruence," 85
India, 48, 108
influence, 41
information
    access to, 35
institutions, 7–8, 17–18
interest groups, 105
Ireland, 25, 48, 50, 61, 92, 108
    cabinet size, 62
    electoral formula, 112, 120
    executive, 23
Israel, 25, 48, 108, 120
    executive, 23
    unicameral legislature, 19
issue dimensions, 129
Italy, 25, 48, 50, 58, 61, 91, 109,
        122, 125
    bicameral legislature, 19
    cabinet size, 62
    constituency size, 108
    constitutional court, 25
    electoral formula, 112
    executive, 23
    metropole-hinterland cleav-
        age, 102
    women's vote, 110

Japan, 25, 108
    bicameral legislature, 19
    electoral formula, 112
    executive, 23
    proportionate system, 49
    reform of electoral system,
        124
    women's vote, 110
Jeffords, Jim, 43
Jospin, Lionel, 68
judge-made law. See common
    law
judicial function, 9–10, 17
judicial independence, 24
judicial review, 11, 15, 25, 30,
        35, 66

judiciary, 9–11, 24, 30
    Anglo-American legal tradi-
        tion, 13
    courts, 12–13, 24–25, 29–30,
        81, 109
    interpretation, 10
jurisdictions, 79–81

Kashmir, 100

latent cleavage, 103–4
Latvia, 92
law, 8. See also statutes
    interpretation of, 13, 24
Lebanon, 100
legal threshold, 112, 127
legislative coalition. See under
        coalition government
legislative defeat. See confi-
        dence
legislative function, 8, 17
legislative government, 64
legislative parties, 40, 126
legislative powers
    division of, 78–82
legislatures, 13, 18
    bicameral, 19–20
    unicameral, 19–20
liberal revolution, 18, 20,
        22. See also Whig
        Revolution of 1688
Lijphart, Arend, 48, 65, 86, 112,
        129
    "incongruence," 85
    on majoritarian and consen-
        sual democracies, 49
    on presidentialism, 38
    on termination of parlia-
        mentary governments,
        54
list systems, 120
Lithuania, 92
Locke, John

separation of powers, 27
Luxembourg, 25, 48, 50, 60–61,
    92
  cabinet ministers, 44
  cabinet size, 62
  electoral formula, 112
  executive, 23

Macdonald, John A., 82
Madison, James, *Federalist Paper
    No.51*, 27–28, 30
Magna Carta, 11
Mahler, Gregory, 77
maintaining the confidence, 32
Major, John, 55–56
majoritarian systems, 47–48, 51,
    54–55, 59, 111
  government formation proc-
    ess, 53
  head of state, 61
majority, 34, 111
  manufactured, 34, 47, 114
  tyranny of the, 41
majority governments, 49
  multi-party, 51
  single-party, 49, 52, 55
  termination, 56, 59
Malaysia, 101
Malta, 48, 61, 92, 122
  electoral formula, 112, 120
Marbury vs. Madison, 30
Marx, Karl, 103–4
mass media, 109
material constitution, 11, 14, 68
metropole-hinterland cleavage,
    102
middle class, 104
minimal winning coalition, 57
minimum connected winning
    coalition, 57
minimum winning coalition,
    57
ministerial government, 64

minority governments, 49
  as exception to the rule, 51
  as "normal politics," 52
  stability of, 50–51
  termination, 56, 59
Mitterand, François, 68–69
mixed government, 27, 38
monarchy, 19, 21–22, 29,
    31–32, 60–61
  absolute, 18, 20
  constitutional, 61
multi-party systems, 47–48, 51,
    70, 111, 125, 127
  stability, 58
municipal or local govern-
    ments, 76

National Assembly (France),
    67, 69
natural hierarchy, 22
Netherlands, 25–26, 48, 50, 61,
    92, 120, 122
  bicameral legislature, 19
  cabinet ministers, 44
  cabinet size, 62
  constituency size, 108
  election (1998), 119
  electoral formula, 112
  executive, 23
New Zealand, 25, 60–61, 123
  as common law country, 14
  constituency size, 108
  electoral formula, 112
  executive, 23
  proportionate system, 49
  reform of electoral system,
    124
  unicameral legislature, 19
  women's vote, 110
No Child Left Behind Act, 84
non-confidence, 87
Northern Ireland
  religious difference, 100

Norway, 25, 48, 50, 55, 61, 122
  cabinet ministers, 44
  cabinet size, 62
  constituency size, 108
  election (1997), 119
  electoral formula, 112
  executive, 23
  unicameral legislature, 19

opposition, 35, 87
ordinal or preferential ballot, 116

Palme, Olaf, 56
paramountcy, 80
"pariah" parties, 53
parliamentary government
    formation, 52–53
  as strong government, 35
  termination, 54–60
parliamentary majority. *See*
    majority governments
parliamentary party, 40, 45, 65
parliamentary supremacy, 31
parliamentary systems, 23,
    26–27, 29, 31–32, 35,
    37–38, 44–70
  cabinets, 61–65
  dual executive, 23, 45
  executive dominance, 34–35,
    63–66
  head of state, 60–61
  presidentialism in, 66–71
partisan politics. *See* party
    system
party-at-large, 40
party discipline, 29, 35, 49,
    63–65, 86
  in presidential systems, 40
  undermining responsible
    government, 34
party government, 64
party system, 40, 45–47, 105,
    107

effective number of parties, 125
effective parties, 129
elective parties, 126
electoral parties, 40
issue dimensions, 129
legislative parties, 40, 126
multi-member constituen-
    cies, 120
multi-party systems, 125
parliamentary party, 40
party-at-large, 40
regional parties, 124–25
right-left ideological scale,
    127–28
strong political parties, 34
two-party system, 115, 124
pluralism, 70
pluralist democracy, 41
plurality electoral systems,
    46–49, 51, 108, 124
  electoral formula, 111
  single member plurality,
    114–16
pocket veto, 42–43
Poland, 60, 70, 92, 108
  election (1997), 119
  executive, 23
polarization, 127
policy compromises, 53–54
policy leverage, 84
policy making, 8, 24, 69
  role of cabinet, 63
political parties. *See* party
    system
popular preference. *See* voter
    preference
popular sovereignty, 27
population, 101
  in center-periphery cleavage,
    102
  control, 11
Portugal, 50, 60–61, 71, 92
  constituency size, 108

constitutional court, 25
electoral formula, 112
executive, 23
proportionate system, 48
post-materialist issue dimen-
    sions, 129
power, 41. *See also* authority
    administrative, 82
    centralization, 73–74
    decentralization, 90
    delegation, 18, 76
    depersonalization, 7
    discretionary, 20–21
    division of, 78–82, 85
    formal, 20
    legislative, 78–82
    private, 41
    territorial distribution of, 74
PR. *See* proportionate electoral
    systems
precedent, 14
President, 29, 66, 68
    chief administrator and head
        of state, 40
    discretionary power, 21–22
    election of, 67
    pre-eminence of, 68
    relation to legislature, 39
    strong, 22–23, 60–61, 70
    veto, 28, 42
    weak, 61
presidentialism, 26, 38–44
    cabinet, 39
    Executive branch staff, 39
    in parliamentary systems,
        67–71
    political executives, 70–71
    "semi-presidential" systems,
        68
Prime Minister, 22–23, 56, 69,
    88
    central figure in cabinet, 61
    as chair of cabinet, 45

discretionary executive
    authority, 33
    as "elected dictator," 49
    head of government, 45
    powers of, 23, 33, 35
    pre-eminence of, 63
prime ministerial government,
    64
private (individual) freedom,
        70. *See also* rights codes
processes, 7
proportionate electoral formula,
    121–22
    list systems, 120
    single transferable vote
        (STV), 120
proportionate electoral systems,
    46–48, 52–54, 108,
    111, 117–20, 122, 127,
    129
    hybrid (mixed-member
        systems), 123–24
    reflection of public opinion,
        125
    second tier, 122–23
provincial jurisdiction, 81
"Public Campaign" (public
    interest group), 109
public opinion, 35, 115, 125
    polling, 109
public policy, 43–44
Putin, Vladimir, 70

quasi-federalism, 77
Quebec
    nationalist aspirations, 80

race, 30, 101
Reagan administration, 83
Reference ("abstract" review),
    25
referendum, 68
    devolution, 90

regionalism or sectionalism, 102, 115
  regional parties, 102, 124–25
reinforcing cleavages, 105
religious difference, 100, 105, 129
representation by population, 20, 29, 85, 107–8
Republican Party's "Contract With America," 42
republicanism, 22, 38
residual clause, 79
responsible government, 29, 32–34, 44–45, 49–50, 63, 65, 87
  impact on party discipline, 40
revolution, 20, 26
Riggs, Fred, 37
right-left ideological scale, 127–28
rights codes, 25
  Bill of Rights, 15, 30
  Charter of Rights and Freedoms, 15
Romania, 92
Roosevelt, Franklin D., 82
rule of law, 24
run-off, 115–16
Russia, 60, 108
  election (1999), 119
  executive, 23

Sainte-Lagüe system, 121–22
Sartori, Giovanni, 38, 68–69, 71
Scandinavian countries
  decentralization, 91
Scotland, 89–90
Scottish people, 101
Senate (Canada), 86
  appointed body, 88
  calls for reform, 89
  patronage chamber, 85
Senate (US), 40, 42

separation of church and state, 100
separation of powers, 15, 18, 22–23, 26–27, 30, 41–42, 60, 71
single executive, 23
single-member plurality (SMP), 114–16
single-member systems, 111
single-party majority government, 49, 52, 55
  termination, 59
single-party minority, 52–53
single transferable vote (STV), 120
Slovakia, 92
Slovenia, 92
SMP. See single-member plurality (SMP)
South Africa
  race, 101
sovereignty, 74–75
  popular, 27
Spain, 61, 90–92, 108
  constitutional court, 25
  election (2000), 119
  electoral formula, 112
  executive, 23
  proportionate system, 48
  women's vote, 110
special autonomy, 91
state
  functions of, 7–11, 14, 17
  head of, 21, 45, 60–61
  levels of, 73
  unitary, 75
Statute of Westminster, 11, 17
statutes, 13–14
strategic voting, 115, 126–27
strong bicameralism, 42, 66, 86–87
strong presidency, 22–23, 60–61, 66, 70

STV. *See* single transferable vote
    (STV)
subnational governments,
    77–78, 85
supranational federalism, 91
supremacy clause, 80
Supreme Court (Canada), 81
    on publication of polls, 109
Supreme Court (US), 25, 29, 81
    landmark civil rights rulings,
      30
    rejection of New Deal
      legislation, 30, 82
Supreme Courts, 12, 14, 25
surplus majority coalition, 57
suspensive veto, 87–88
Sweden, 25–26, 48, 50, 55, 61,
    92, 109, 122
    cabinet size, 62
    constituency size, 108
    election (1998), 119
    electoral formula, 112
    executive, 23
    unicameral legislature, 19
    women's vote, 110
Swedish Social Democratic
    Party, 51
Switzerland, 25, 48, 56, 58, 61,
    66
    bicameral legislature, 19
    as confederation, 79
    constitutional amending
      formula, 16–17
    election (1999), 119
    electoral formula, 112
    ethno-linguistic cleavages,
      101
    strong bicameralism, 86
    women's vote, 110

television, 109
termination of governments,
    54–60

dissolution, 54
    electoral reasons, 59
    political reasons, 59–60
Thatcher, Margaret
    caucus revolt, 56
transfer payments, 83–84
two-party system, 48, 115, 124

Uganda, 101
Ukraine, 60
unicameral legislatures, 19–20
unified executive. *See under*
    executives
unitary states (definition), 75
United Kingdom, 25, 33, 48,
    50, 61, 92, 111
    bicameral legislature, 19–20
    cabinet size, 62
    common law, 14
    constituency size, 108
    constitution, 11–12, 31
    cultural differences, 101
    election (1997), 118
    electoral formula, 112
    executive, 23
    home rule, 90
    House of Lords, 88
    Law Lords, 28
    parliamentary system, 26, 53
    Privy Council, 32
    as unitary state, 75
    women's vote, 110
United States, 25, 66, 73,
    76–77, 83, 85, 111
    Administration, 39
    bicameral legislature, 19
    Bill of Rights, 15, 30
    cabinet secretaries, 39
    as common law country, 14
    Congress, 28–29, 86
    constituency size, 108
    constitution, 13, 26–27, 37,
      76, 79

amending formula, 15–17, 28

amendments, 79, 81

from decentralized to centralized federation, 80

"elastic clause," 79

electoral formula, 112

electoral participation, 106

executive, 23

franchise, 107–8

government (as weak government), 30

importance of the judiciary, 30

judicial review, 25, 30

legislature, 28

limitation of states' rights, 81

military solutions, 40

party system, 29, 115

political advertising, 109

popular sovereignty, 27

President, 21

election of, 38

international prominence, 21

term of office, 29, 41

presidential system, 26, 28

race, 101

representation by population, 20

Senate, 40, 42

separation of church and state, 100

separation of powers, 15, 18, 22–23, 26–27, 30, 41–42, 60, 71

strong bicameralism, 86

Supremacy Clause, 80

Supreme Court, 25, 28–30, 81–82

terms of office, 29

transfer payments, 84

urban-rural cleavages, 103

women's vote, 107, 110

universal adult suffrage, 110

urban-rural cleavages, 102–3, 129

Venezuela, 70

veto, 21, 28, 43, 86–87

pocket, 42–43

suspensive, 87–88

voter preference, 116, 124, 129–30

voter turnout, 44

Wales, 89–90

Walesa, Lech, 70

Welsh people, 101

Whig Revolution of 1688, 31–33

"winner-take-all. *See* plurality electoral systems

women's vote, 107

Yeltsin, Boris, 70